COOK BEAUTIFUL

COOK BEAUTIFUL

ATHENA CALDERONE

CREATOR OF EYESWOON

—

PHOTOGRAPHY BY JOHNNY MILLER

ABRAMS, NEW YORK

For Victor and Jivan.
You are the foundation to my life—my greatest champions,
truest confidants, and most treasured teachers. Our little family is my gold,
my heart, my greatest success, my everything.

FALL

WINTER

INTRODUCTION

Food is our greatest unifier; something we can all relate to, no matter our backgrounds, passions, or palates. The act of breaking bread draws us together emotionally, connecting us to our loved ones and our pasts. A shared meal nourishes so much more than our bodies—it feeds our souls. It ignites our senses. It evokes a time and place we long to hold on to and remember.

My love of food truly brought my entire life into focus. I've followed many paths, from acting in my twenties to interior design in my thirties. But it wasn't until I embraced my love of cooking, that I found the missing piece of my creative puzzle. Finding my voice through food took time, effort, and a lot of trial and error, but it also offered me the ability to be open: to new ideas, to tried-and-true methods, and to my own creative instincts. The kitchen became a space for invention, a workshop, and a studio. It made all of my artistic fragments finally fit together into one unified vision. That vision, EyeSwoon, is the site I've dedicated to—you guessed it—all the things that make my eyes swoon. It's where I cook, style, and write, sharing everything from design inspiration and recipes to entertaining tips. EyeSwoon began in 2011 as a way for me to chronicle my own creative journey in the hope that it would inspire a journey for others. With this book, that voyage continues.

A FEAST FOR THE EYES

My path has been far from typical. I'm not a culinary school grad and I've never worked in a restaurant kitchen. But I'm super curious by nature and always eager to learn. EyeSwoon has given me the opportunity to cook with culinary gods like Jean-Georges Vongerichten and Jody Williams and work alongside so many crazy-talented photographers, home cooks, and food bloggers. The past five years have given me plenty to absorb!

I suppose what sets my story apart from most self-trained cooks is that my eyes, as much as my taste buds, guide me in the kitchen. My true passion—what really makes me swoon—is creating beauty. Aesthetics guide me in everything I do, whether I'm hunting for the most vibrant vegetables at the farmer's market or setting a stunning table. I attribute my reverence for aesthetics to my mother. When I was a child, she would turn the most ordinary events into unforgettable experiences by paying special attention to the way things looked, felt, or tasted. I remember the ritual of setting the Thanksgiving table:

We spent hours laying out her favorite black-and-white china, pressing the linens, and setting out the candles . . . and still, the turkey was perfect.

So it's no surprise, then, that I believe food just tastes better when it's beautiful and made with love. It's the reason that I strive to create a feast for the senses every time I cook. While taste and smell are obviously paramount to how we perceive a meal, visual cues are just as important. Before a single bite passes our lips, our brains are working out an answer to the question: Does this look good to me? Whether we're at home or a restaurant, we all eat with our eyes. A beautiful plate of food has emotional power and wholly undeniable magic—and my goal is to help you capture that.

RED SAUCE ROOTS

I was raised in an Italian-American family in Nassau County, Long Island. Although it was only thirty minutes from Manhattan, it may as well have been its own universe. In our house, family and meals were synonymous, never more so than on Sundays, when the entire extended clan gathered. Our Sunday classic was pasta with red sauce. Pasta was always called "macaroni," regardless of its shape, and the sauce was always filled with braciole, sausage, and meatballs. There was always ricotta (Polly-O, never fresh) and a lot of garlic bread.

Though nothing was particularly sophisticated—we ate frozen corn in the winter and cooked our broccoli until it took on a grayish hue—those meals, with their love and boisterous energy, still loom large in my heart as my happiest childhood memories.

After college, I moved to New York and worked as a model and bartender. One fateful night while I was behind the bar, I met a young DJ named Victor Calderone. I was twenty-two when we fell in love, and twenty-four when we got married. Two years later, I was pregnant with our son, Jivan. While most of my friends were focused on their careers or having wild nights out with boys, here I was, a yoga-obsessed twenty-six-year-old with a baby on my hip, unsure of what my future held where my career was concerned. But I did know one thing: Boy oh boy, did I love my little trio of a family. And learning how to feed them well seemed like a natural way to express that feeling.

FINDING COMFORT IN THE KITCHEN

Though we had a beautiful kitchen, I had barely turned on the oven until I was pregnant with Jivan; it was only then, wanting to be a proper homemaker, that I started baking.

The precision and science of my new pastime appealed to my perfectionist streak, and also fueled my creativity. As I continued to learn and experiment, the kitchen became my sanctuary, a place that was as surprising as it was comforting. I'd roll out pastry, pump up the music, and sing along as I went into discovery mode, riffing on new flavors and techniques—and having a lot of fun in the process. Since I had a newborn and Victor was often traveling for work, I began inviting friends over to keep me company. I whipped up simple dinners, and while Jivan slept, we enjoyed the fruits of my labor. Soon, cooking became both my creative and my social outlet.

There was no question I was blessed with a beautiful home life. But I felt that career-wise, I was "doing it all wrong." I had so much creative energy bursting inside of me, but no matter what I tried—acting, poetry, yoga, fashion styling, singing, dance—I couldn't figure out where to direct it. To be "successful," I thought, you had to be just one thing. And so the question remained: What was I meant to offer?

Victor's career, meanwhile, was taking off. He started working all over the world, and Jivan and I tagged along. Those trips were an education: They opened my eyes to new flavors, cultures, architecture, and design. In Morocco, I trawled the *souks* for rugs and learned to appreciate texture and patina through the new textiles and materials I found. In Spain, I was introduced to the small-plates concept at local tapas bars. In Greece, I sat at a tiny beach shack and worked up the nerve to try octopus for the first time—no small feat for someone who grew up petrified of eating fish!

Although I didn't know it at the time, all of this traveling, homemaking, and mommy-ing was in fact leading me somewhere. I channeled all of the inspiration from my travels into trying new things in my kitchen and designing our loft. I commissioned furniture, hunted for the perfect textiles, and obsessed over color schemes and floor plans. My design sense caught the eye of my friend John Rawlins, who encouraged me to study interior design at Parsons School of Design. I took his advice and eventually, we decided to open our own firm, Rawlins Calderone Design, in 2006.

Though interior décor certainly filled a creative void, it didn't speak to all of my passions; something was still missing. Around that time, the dinner parties I'd been hosting grew into more elaborate gatherings. I began creating overall experiences that went beyond just the food, inspiring a distinct mood with table settings, color palettes, and flowers. The more I cooked, the more confidence I gained. It wasn't long before I realized that those nights when my guests were gathered around the kitchen island as I chop-chop-chopped were the swooniest moments in my life.

What had started as an interest quickly turned into an obsession. I passed hours dissecting recipes on Epicurious, read countless cookbooks like novels, and signed up for classes at the Institute for Culinary Education and the French Culinary Institute. Brooklyn restaurants—which at the time were just beginning to boom—became a huge source of inspiration. After a dinner out, I'd often spend the better part of the next day in the kitchen, attempting to re-create a dish I'd fallen in love with the night before. And thanks to the local farmer's markets, I began to think more about cooking seasonally. As I spent more time behind the stove, the parallels between my approach to cooking and design became apparent to me. Both touched upon my love of creating beauty; of seeking harmony in opposing flavors, textures, and hues; of looking for that slightly unexpected element. I longed to find an outlet that would unite them, but had no clue what that might be.

A SITE IS BORN

I can distinctly recall the summer of 2011: I had just completed the design and renovation of our Amagansett home. There was so much newness and excitement in our community, and my homemaking side was in full swing. Because I was constantly hosting friends and family in my new beach house, I had an abundance of recipes. And because I'd spent the prior year sourcing natural materials and salvaged oddities for our space, I had a wealth of design information. And so that September, I decided to share it all with friends on a Tumblr page I titled EyeSwoon. I was far from a techie. I had barely picked up a camera, let alone photographed food. And I had zero writing experience. But none of that mattered: EyeSwoon immediately became a home for all of my overlapping passions. I dove into the concept and, before long, found myself balancing precariously on a stepladder in my kitchen, camera in one hand and whisk in the other, to capture the perfect shot. I was learning every day, and I'd never been happier. Finally, in my late thirties, I felt like I'd arrived where I was always meant to be. Rather than being embarrassed by my creative ramblings, I could celebrate them all in one place.

EyeSwoon has since evolved from a sideline into a full-on career. It really found its voice when I began featuring the tastemakers and culinary geniuses who inspire me; in the process, I built a following, and finally felt rooted in a community. I'd enter someone's kitchen as a stranger and walk out with a new friend—we were united in our passion for food and beauty.

SIMPLE IDEAS, THOUGHTFULLY EXECUTED

Beautiful, by the way, does not necessarily mean *complicated.* My own style is rooted in simplicity; while aesthetics are paramount to me, so is accessibility. That's why I've developed an arsenal of easy tricks over the years for making food that's not only delicious, but also a feast for the eyes. Those tricks reflect this book's core philosophy, which is that with a little thoughtful planning, you can execute simple ideas that appear to be far more sophisticated or difficult than they actually are.

Oddly, this more visual side of food has been largely ignored by books aimed at the home cook, which is why we so often hear that a dish "didn't turn out like the picture." I'm here to change that. Every recipe in my book is accompanied by a photograph—because let's face it, I wouldn't dream of trying a new recipe without a gorgeous visual to lure me in. And what's more unique is that each recipe will include a "Swoon Tip," in which I spill my secrets for making food look as good as it tastes. I offer advice on everything from prepping to presentation, from the best methods for slicing veggies to the prettiest ways to plate your culinary creations. I'll explain why giving your blanched snap peas a quick ice bath is the key to keeping them vibrant green, why bringing your steak to room temperature is essential to getting a gorgeous golden sear, and why sometimes an artful mess of food is more appealing than a neatly composed plate. Some of these strategies I've picked up on my own, through trial and error; others I've learned from the many food bloggers, stylists, and top chefs I've had the honor of cooking alongside over the years. Passing along this kind of insight was part of my mission when I started EyeSwoon—like I said, I'm a sharer by nature!

A GIRL FOR ALL SEASONS

While this book is an extension of EyeSwoon, it's also a meditation on the way the seasons inform not only our ingredients and cooking styles but also the look and feel of our gatherings. Just as the flavors we crave change with the weather, our mood shifts and so does the aesthetic we long to surround ourselves with. To best reflect that idea, I've organized this book by season, each of which concludes with a tablescape, inspired by what's happening in the natural world. On the pages that follow, I break down the décor into practical advice on linens, flowers, clever place settings, and thoughtful homemade touches for your guests to take home.

MY COOKING STYLE

All of which brings me, of course, to the food, which is bright, fresh, and approachable. No matter the recipe, my goal is always to build robust flavors with minimal, basic ingredients and a little know-how. I'm a stickler for using the best peak-season ingredients—farmer's market veggies, day-boat seafood, excellent olive oil—and I try not to undermine their essential magic with too much fuss.

Lemon, chile, and fresh herbs are my kitchen's holy trinity, and Mediterranean influences dominate. Texture is essential to my food: I love the crunch of a nut or bread crumb. I use herby sauces to finish my meats and fishes, and adore a salty shave of fresh cheese and the briny tang of an olive or caper. Many of these flavors show up again and again, and for good reason: As you'll see, they can enrich your food in so many ways. Likewise, chimichurri, pesto, salsa verde, gremolata, and relishes are used in abundance because I just can't help myself. They are just so swoony, and so useful for brightening flavors throughout the year.

It can be intimidating to create delicious, enticing food and set a gorgeous table. I want to show you that it doesn't have to be—all you need is a little forethought and a few simple techniques. Creating a stunning meal is about so much more than what meets the eye: It's about building community, and making ordinary gatherings feel like celebrations. I get so much joy from cooking and sitting down to eat with friends; it floods me with that "Sunday dinner" warmth so evocative of my red sauce roots. So, here's to creating lasting experiences and memories through beauty. Come with me—let's swoon!

SPRING

WHEN I WAS GROWING UP, words like *seasonal* and *locally sourced* may as well have been a foreign language. We didn't think much about which vegetables were being harvested just a few miles from our suburban home, or which fruits were reaching their perfect juicy peak on the trees of Long Island's orchards. In my family, we ate frozen corn in the winter and bought our tomatoes—usually flown in from California—at the Key Foods all year long.

What changed that mindset, for me, was discovering New York City's greenmarkets. That first fresh, sugary-sweet pea, popped from the pod and eaten raw—right there in the veggie stall—sent me swooning. Shopping seasonally made me increasingly attuned to the way produce shifts from month to month, and those changes now inform the way I cook.

Starting in mid-April, after dropping my son off at school, I often head to Union Square, where New York City's largest greenmarket is in full swing four days a week. After enduring months of brutal cold, I feel as though I've come alive again, right in sync with the tender shoots pushing their way through the thawing earth. I'm always in awe at the lush transition: Whereas just a month earlier, the stalls were filled with potato after potato, suddenly there are bright green fava beans, ramps, and asparagus. I tend to get a little carried away and buy too much. Some people spring clean, but I spring market!

This time of year we crave something lighter than winter's long braises and cozy flavors, but haven't reached the point of completely avoiding the oven. We want the best of both worlds, the raw *and* the cooked. For lunch, I might pull out my mandoline and slice up paper-thin wisps of raw fennel for a vibrant salad. For dinner, I might roast asparagus and radishes, dousing them in a tangy mustard sauce.

As April turns to May, my family begins to spend more time at our home in Amagansett, where I plant my herb garden, nestling the little plants into the fertile soil. I always seem to hurry home from the nursery and dig right in with my hands, emerging a few hours later happy as a clam despite my mud-splattered white jeans and the clods of earth stuck under every nail.

When I'm not tending to my own (very modest) crop, I love to spend time at Amber Waves, the picturesque, eight-acre organic farm where I collect my weekly CSA box. I catch up with the farmers and explore the fields, picking the first dainty strawberries and snipping fragrant lavender sprigs. I always leave inspired by the energy invested in growing this beautiful food—and feeling a renewed sense of connection to the community I'm so lucky to be a part of. And of course, I can't resist sharing my spoils with friends. Perhaps I jump the gun a bit by firing up the grill at the first hint of warm weather, but spring lamb chops practically beg to be flame kissed. I invite a crowd, fill the house with blooming quince branches, open the windows, and breathe deep. Finally, it's spring.

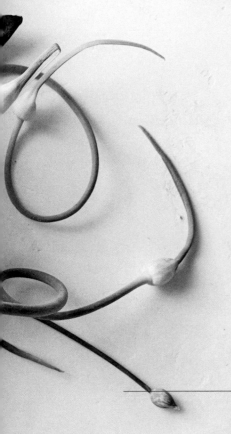

IN SEASON

APRICOTS	DILL	RAMPS
ARTICHOKES	ENDIVE	RHUBARB
ARUGULA	FAVA BEANS	SPINACH
ASPARAGUS	FENNEL	SPRING ONIONS
CHERRIES	MINT	STRAWBERRIES
CHIVES	MORELS	WATERCRESS
	PEAS	
	RADISHES	

SPINACH AND GOAT CHEESE FRITTATA

Starting in late spring, I tend to have a steady stream of friends staying at my house in Amagansett, so I've learned to embrace an all-day mindset when it comes to entertaining. Guests appreciate a beautiful breakfast just as much as—if not more than—a fancy dinner. Frittata is one of my favorites. Fast and easy, it's a great vehicle for showcasing spring greens—and using up leftovers from the night before. If you're pressed for time, frittata can be made ahead and served room temperature. Just spruce it up with a handful of torn herbs before serving. Feel free to sub zucchini for the spinach here, or replace goat cheese with ricotta. And spare yourself the anxiety of getting the finished dish to release perfectly onto a platter—I slice mine directly in the cast-iron pan.

SERVES 6

—

½ pound (225 g) baby potatoes
  (6 to 8)

10 large eggs

⅓ cup (75 ml) crème fraîche

¾ teaspoon kosher salt

3 tablespoons extra-virgin olive oil

1 leek, white and pale green parts
  only, halved lengthwise, rinsed, and
  thinly sliced crosswise

1 spring onion or scallion, thinly sliced

Salt and freshly cracked pepper

2 cups (40 g) lightly packed baby
  spinach

3 ounces (85 g) goat cheese

FOR GARNISH

1 handful fresh parsley or cilantro

1 handful chopped fresh dill

1 handful chopped chives,
  with blossoms, if available

½ lemon, zested

Preheat the oven to 350°F (175°C). In a saucepan, boil the potatoes until fork tender. Drain and when they are cool enough to handle, thinly slice the potatoes.

Whisk together the eggs, crème fraîche, and salt.

In a cast-iron or nonstick 10-inch ovenproof skillet, heat the oil over medium heat. Add the leek and onion and sauté until soft and translucent, 4 to 5 minutes. Add the potatoes and cook another few minutes. Season with salt and pepper. Stir in the spinach and cook just until wilted. Lower the heat to medium-low and pour in the egg mixture. Cook for a few minutes, pushing the eggs toward the center of the skillet as they cook. As you work, be careful not to break apart the potatoes. Once the eggs have set on the bottom, dot the top of the frittata with goat cheese. Place the skillet in the oven and cook just until the frittata has set, 12 to 15 minutes.

Remove the frittata from the oven and cool slightly. To serve, garnish with fresh herbs and lemon zest.

swoon tip

Fine herbs like dill, chives, and cilantro bruise easily under a knife, so rather than putting them on the chopping block, trim them with a pair of scissors. Here, snip them directly over the frittata, from higher above than you might think, allowing them to cascade in an artfully haphazard manner.

SMOKED SALMON TOAST
WITH RED ONION AND HERBS

Little toasts are one of my favorite nibbles to serve guests, and of all the many varieties I've put together over the years, this is the one that gets gobbled with the most ferocity. People go crazy over smoked salmon! Of course, the appeal here goes beyond the fish—there's also the cooling lemon crème fraîche, the sharp, tangy pickled onion, and the refreshingly crunchy cukes. The elements truly harmonize. On weekends when I suspect I'll have friends around, I often make the components in advance so these toasts can be assembled in a pinch for an elegant, impromptu brunch.

MAKES 4 TOASTS
—

FOR THE PICKLED ONION

½ cup (120 ml) cider vinegar

1 tablespoon honey

1 teaspoon coriander seeds

1 teaspoon kosher salt

1 small red onion, thinly sliced

FOR THE LEMON CRÈME FRAÎCHE

½ cup (120 ml) crème fraîche

1 lemon, grated zest and 1 tablespoon juice

Salt and freshly cracked pepper

FOR THE TOAST

4 slices good-quality crusty bread, such as whole-wheat sourdough or pumpernickel

Extra-virgin olive oil, for drizzling

1 (4-ounce/115-g) package smoked salmon

2 Persian cucumbers, sliced into ¼-inch-thick (6-mm-thick) rounds

1½ tablespoons capers

1 small handful fresh dill, torn

1 small handful fresh mint, torn

Chive blossom flowers

Freshly cracked pepper

Lemon wedges, for serving (optional)

Make the pickled onion: In a small saucepan, bring the vinegar, honey, coriander seeds, and salt to a boil. Place the onions in a nonreactive bowl. Slowly pour the hot liquid over the onions and cool to room temperature. Refrigerate until ready to use. Stored in a well-sealed container, onions will keep in the refrigerator for up to two weeks.

Make the lemon crème fraîche: Whisk together the crème fraîche and lemon zest and juice. Season with salt and pepper.

Make the toast: Preheat the grill over medium-high heat to about 400°F (250°C). Lightly drizzle both sides of the bread with oil. Grill until lightly charred, 2 to 3 minutes per side. Top with the lemon crème fraîche, smoked salmon, cucumbers, capers, and a few pickled red onions. Scatter with fresh herbs, chive blossom flowers, and a few grinds of pepper. Serve with lemon wedges on the side, if desired.

swoon tip

Invest in a 99-cent spritz bottle and wake up tired-looking microgreens by misting them before adding them to the dish. Unlike heartier greens, their dainty and delicate leaves will wilt, rather than perk up, if submerged in ice water.

GRILLED ZUCCHINI FLATBREAD
WITH RAMP-PISTACHIO PESTO

The appearance of ramps at the farmer's market is often the first sign that spring has sprung. And thanks in part to their short season, from late April until very early June, they tend to set off a bit of a culinary frenzy. The trendiest veggie since kale, this green queen is actually a long, wild spring onion—and, in terms of flavor, it packs a deliciously garlicky punch. I try to make the most of ramps while they're around, using them in everything from frittatas to pestos—including this one, which I love to slather on my homemade flatbread. Brightened by lemon and mellowed a bit by rich, crunchy pistachios, it's just the right foil for sweet and smoky charred zucchini.

SERVES 6 TO 8
—

FOR THE PESTO
12 ounces (340 g) ramps
2 tablespoons unsalted butter
¼ cup (25 g) grated Parmigiano-
  Reggiano
¾ cup (180 ml) extra-virgin olive oil
1½ teaspoons kosher salt
2 tablespoons fresh lemon juice
½ cup (65 g) unsalted pistachios,
  toasted and roughly chopped, divided

FOR THE ZUCCHINI
2 medium zucchini, cut on a bias into
  ½-inch (12-mm) slices
Extra-virgin olive oil, for drizzling
½ teaspoon smoked paprika
Salt and freshly cracked pepper

FOR SERVING
Grilled flatbread (page 270)
1 handful fresh mint, finely chopped
1 handful sunflower sprouts, stems
  trimmed
Flaky sea salt

Make the pesto: Trim the roots from the ramps and pull off the thin membrane that covers the bulb. Rinse thoroughly under cold water. Cut the leafy green tops from the bulbs and set aside.

Bring a small saucepan of salted water up to a simmer over medium-low heat. While the water heats, prepare an ice bath and have it ready by the stove. Add the ramp greens to the saucepan and cook for 30 seconds. Using tongs, remove the greens and plunge them into the ice bath. Once they've cooled, drain them thoroughly.

In a medium saucepan, melt the butter over medium heat. Add the ramp bulbs and sauté for about 2 minutes or until softened, being careful not to let them brown.

Transfer the ramp greens, bulbs, cheese, olive oil, salt, and lemon juice to the bowl of a food processor. Add ¼ cup (32 g) of the pistachios. Pulse until a smooth pesto forms. You should have about 2⅓ cups (555 ml), but will only use about half for the flatbread. The remaining pesto can be stored in an airtight container and refrigerated for 3 days. To help maintain its color, drizzle it with a little olive oil or place a piece of plastic wrap directly on its surface. You can spread the leftover pesto on a sandwich, stir it into pasta, or use it as a dip.

Make the zucchini: Preheat the grill over medium-high heat to about 400°F (205°C). Drizzle the zucchini with oil. Sprinkle with paprika and season generously with salt and pepper, tossing until the zucchini is evenly coated. Grill until the zucchini is cooked through and lightly charred on both sides, about 8 minutes total.

Spread the pesto over a grilled flatbread, leaving a ½-inch (12-mm) border around the edges. Top with the zucchini, mint, sunflower sprouts, and remaining ¼ cup (32 g) pistachios. Drizzle with oil and sprinkle with flaky sea salt.

While I'm all for embracing a rainbow of produce in my cooking, sometimes I prefer to pick a single hue and hammer it home. Here, green sauce meets a texturally diverse array of green toppings—zucchini, pistachios, mint, and sprouts—for a dish as verdant as spring itself. The secret to my pesto's vibrant hue: shocking the blanched ramps in ice water after cooking them.

THE SPRINGIEST SPRING SALAD

Highlighting the season's daintiest delights—watercress, pea shoots, tender herbs—this salad is such a welcome change of pace after the muddled and muted flavors of winter. Making it relies heavily on a mandoline, so I encourage you to buy one if the tool isn't already part of your arsenal. The lemon vinaigrette is a variation on my go-to dressing, with crème fraîche lending some welcome richness to the light, crunchy veg. Feel free to ad-lib with whatever looks best at the farmer's market—endive, watermelon radish, and snaps peas would all work beautifully here. But whatever you do, don't skimp on the fresh tarragon; its tender leaves add a complex anise-like flavor that really rounds out the dish.

SERVES 4

—

FOR THE VINAIGRETTE

¼ cup (60 ml) fresh lemon juice

1 orange, grated zest and juice

3 tablespoons crème fraîche

2 teaspoons Dijon mustard

1 teaspoon honey

½ cup (120 ml) extra-virgin olive oil

1 teaspoon kosher salt

Freshly cracked pepper

1 tablespoon chopped fresh chives

1 tablespoon chopped fresh tarragon

FOR THE SALAD

1 fennel bulb, quartered, cored, and thinly shaved on a mandoline, fronds reserved

1 green radish, thinly shaved on a mandoline

1 bunch watercress

1 cup (145 g) shelled peas, blanched and shocked

1 handful pea greens or pea shoots

¼ cup (30 g) toasted pistachios, roughly chopped

Chive or pea shoot blossoms, for serving

Flaky sea salt, for serving

Make the vinaigrette: Whisk together the lemon and orange juice, crème fraîche, mustard, and honey. In a slow, steady stream, whisk in the oil until emulsified. Season with salt and pepper and stir in the fresh herbs.

Make the salad: Toss the fennel, radish, watercress, and peas with just enough vinaigrette to lightly coat them. Transfer to a serving platter. Top with the pea greens, pistachios, reserved fennel fronds, chive blossom flowers, and a light sprinkle of flaky sea salt.

swoon tip The earth feels so fertile in spring—even the herbs are bursting into flower. Garnishing with a few blooming beauties—here, I used chive and pea shoot blossoms—is an almost effortless way to prettify a salad. Keep an eye out for them at the farmer's markets, and don't feel you have to pile them on—just a few will do.

GRILLED BABY ARTICHOKES WITH HERBED AIOLI

I have a soft spot for artichokes. As a child, I considered these spiky vegetables to be "adult food," so the fact that I enjoyed eating them made me feel so sophisticated and grown up. Etched in my memory is the ritual my father and I always shared: After plucking off and scraping my teeth against each and every petal, I'd carefully spoon away the artichoke's fuzzy center and proudly present the heart to my dad—it's his favorite part. Here, baby artichokes—which aren't actually babies at all, but just smaller buds that grow low down on the plant—are simply grilled and served with a garlic aioli. Classic and delicious.

SERVES 6 TO 8

—

FOR THE AIOLI

1 clove garlic

¾ teaspoon kosher salt

1 teaspoon Dijon mustard

1 egg yolk

2 teaspoons fresh lemon juice

½ cup (120 ml) canola oil

¼ cup (60 ml) extra-virgin olive oil

2 tablespoons finely chopped fresh herbs such as tarragon, chives, or parsley

FOR THE ARTICHOKES

4 lemons, divided

4 pounds (1.8 kg) baby artichokes

2 bay leaves

Kosher salt

Extra-virgin olive oil, for drizzling

Salt and freshly cracked pepper

Chopped fresh herbs, for serving

Make the aioli: Using a mortar and pestle, mash the garlic and salt into a paste. Add the mustard and continue to mash until a smooth paste forms. Transfer the mixture to a small bowl and whisk in the egg yolk and lemon juice. Whisk in both oils in a slow, steady stream until the aioli has emulsified and thickened. Stir in the herbs and taste and adjust for seasoning. If you're not using the aioli immediately, cover and keep it refrigerated.

Make the artichokes: Fill a large bowl with cold water. Using a vegetable peeler, peel the rind from two of the lemons into strips and reserve. Cut the peeled lemons in half, squeeze the juice into the bowl of water, and place the squeezed halves in the water.

Using a sharp knife, peel off the artichoke's tough outer leaves until you've reached the tender inner leaves. Peel and trim the artichoke stem, then cut the artichoke in half lengthwise. Place in the lemon water to prevent browning. Repeat with the remaining artichokes.

Fill a large pot about halfway with cold water. Add the strips of lemon zest, bay leaves, and a large pinch of salt. Bring to a boil, then add the artichokes. Reduce the heat and simmer until the artichokes are fork tender, 5 to 6 minutes. Drain the artichokes and transfer to a bowl. Drizzle with olive oil and season with salt and pepper, tossing to evenly coat.

Preheat the grill over medium-high heat to about 400°F (205°C). Grill the artichokes, cut-side down, in a single layer until they form nice, dark grill marks, 5 to 6 minutes. Flip and grill the second side until lightly charred, about 3 minutes. Quarter the two remaining lemons and grill until charred, 2 to 3 minutes. Finish the artichokes with a sprinkle of fresh herbs and a squeeze of juice from the grilled lemons. Serve warm with the herbed aioli.

Artichokes are flowers, after all, and just like the blooms that decorate your table, they require a little extra TLC to keep them looking their best. To prevent their sculptural petals from turning murky brown, drop the artichokes into a big bowl of lemon water as soon as they're trimmed.

SUGAR SNAP PEA AND FAVA SALAD WITH BUFFALO MOZZARELLA

Yes, it's true: Favas are higher maintenance than your average bean. First, they have to be popped out of their pods, then blanched and slipped from their thick individual skins. But the reward here far outweighs the drudgery—especially when you approach the prep as a meditation, setting yourself up somewhere comfy and zoning out as you peel. With their creamy texture, favas are a pleasure unto themselves, but they also play well with other seasonal crops, like the spring onions, sugar snaps, and soft herbs that round out this super-fresh salad. The addition of buffalo mozzarella gives the dish a decadent feel, making it substantial enough for a light meal. Sometimes, when I'm craving a little extra crunch, I also sprinkle on some homemade bread crumbs. (See page 269 for a recipe.) And if you can't find favas—or they prove to be too much work—just swap in some defrosted frozen edamame. I won't tell.

SERVES 4

—

8 ounces (225 g) sugar snap peas, trimmed and blanched (about 2 cups/120 g)

1½ cups (255 g) blanched and shelled fava beans

2 spring onions, white and pale green parts only, thinly sliced

1 large handful baby arugula

1 small bunch fresh mint, roughly torn

1 small bunch fresh basil, roughly torn

1 lemon, grated zest and juice

1½ tablespoons champagne or white wine vinegar

Extra-virgin olive oil, for drizzling

1 ball buffalo mozzarella or burrata cheese (about 8 ounces/225 g)

Flaky sea salt and freshly cracked pepper, for serving

Toss together the snap peas, favas, spring onions, arugula, mint, and basil. Lightly drizzle with lemon juice, vinegar, and a bit of oil. Toss to combine. Gently tear the cheese and place it on a serving platter. Plate the greens on top of or alongside the cheese. Sprinkle with flaky salt, lemon zest, and a few twists of pepper.

swoon tip Ever wonder how to keep your snap peas dazzling green? The answer lies in blanching and shocking. It's all about timing here, so it's essential to have your ice bath ready before you add the peas to the pot. And forget about draining the veg in a colander—you run the risk of overcooking and dulling their hue. Instead, scoop them out with a slotted spoon or skimmer after just about thirty seconds of boiling and immediately dunk them in the freezing cold water to stop the cooking.

ROASTED ASPARAGUS AND RADISHES WITH MUSTARD-TARRAGON VINAIGRETTE

Here's a bit of asparagus trivia: Did you know that if you simply bend an asparagus stalk, it will snap in exactly the right place every single time, separating the tough end from the tender shoot? Clearly, I'm a geek because this nugget of information got me crazy excited! And once I snapped, I never went back. Now I ask just about every cook I know if they cut or snap. If you're not already a snapper, definitely give it a go here; the technique makes this dead-simple side dish even easier to throw together. It's a recipe that my whole family loves, and with its pink-and-green color scheme it looks like a million bucks on the plate. Thanks to a tarragon-spiked champagne vinaigrette, it tastes just as lively.

SERVES 4 TO 6

—

1 bunch radishes, trimmed and halved, quartered if large

1 bunch asparagus (about 1 pound/ 455 g), trimmed

Extra-virgin olive oil for drizzling, plus 3 tablespoons

Salt and freshly cracked pepper

1½ tablespoons champagne vinegar

1½ tablespoons whole-grain mustard

4 to 5 sprigs fresh tarragon, leaves removed

Preheat the oven to 425°F (220°C).

Spread the radishes on a baking sheet and the asparagus on a second baking sheet. Drizzle both with oil and season with salt and pepper, tossing to evenly coat the vegetables. Spread the vegetables in an even, single layer.

Roast the radishes for 10 minutes. Give them a shake, then add the pan of asparagus to the oven. Roast until both the radishes and asparagus are lightly golden and tender, 12 to 14 minutes.

While the vegetables are roasting, whisk together the vinegar and mustard, then slowly whisk in the 3 tablespoons oil. Season to taste with salt and pepper.

Transfer the radishes and asparagus to a serving platter. Lightly drizzle with the vinaigrette and sprinkle with tarragon. Serve immediately with extra vinaigrette on the side.

swoon tip

You know what they say—if you've got it, flaunt it. Emphasize the natural beauty of those ravishing radishes by leaving on a quarter-inch of their green tops when trimming. And although the recipe doesn't demand them, get your hands on breakfast radishes if you can—their elongated shape is gorgeous here.

ZUCCHINI AND FETA FRITTERS
WITH AVOCADO CREAM

Fritters always remind me of my paternal grandmother. When I was a kid, she'd make a killer corn and zucchini version that I'd gobble up by the half dozen, slathering them with sour cream. These savory little pancakes build on her legacy, with a few adjustments. For one, I've traded sour cream for a citrusy avocado dipping sauce. It's ridiculously smooth—almost like cake frosting—and just tart enough to cut through the richness of the fried veg. The trick to extra-crisp patties is to remove as much moisture as possible from the grated zucchini before cooking.

MAKES 10 FRITTERS

—

2 medium zucchini (about 1 pound/
   455 g total), coarsely grated

3 scallions, white and light green
   parts only, thinly sliced, plus more
   for serving

½ cup (25 g) lightly packed fresh
   parsley, roughly chopped

¼ cup (13 g) chopped fresh dill, plus
   more for serving

1 large egg

1 egg yolk

⅓ cup (75 ml) all-purpose flour

Salt and freshly cracked pepper

¾ cup (115 g) crumbled Bulgarian
   feta

¼ cup (60 ml) canola oil

¼ cup (60 ml) extra-virgin olive oil

Avocado cream (page 268), for serving

Flaky sea salt, for serving

Place the grated zucchini in a clean kitchen towel and sprinkle it with a good pinch of salt, then twist the towel to squeeze out excess water. Twist two to three times to remove as much water as possible. Turn the zucchini into a large bowl and mix with the scallions, parsley, dill, egg, and egg yolk. Add the flour, stirring slowly so that no lumps form. Season with salt and pepper. Gently fold in the feta and set aside.

In a large sauté pan, heat about half of the canola and half of the olive oil over medium heat. Working in batches, drop ¼ cupfuls (20 g) of the zucchini mixture into the pan, leaving about 2 inches between each fritter. Fry until golden and crisp, 1½ to 2 minutes per side. Transfer the fritters to a paper towel–lined plate. Repeat with the remaining mixture, adding additional oil as needed. Serve the fritters sprinkled with flaky sea salt, thinly sliced scallions, and chopped dill, with the avocado cream on the side.

Rather than transferring these golden morsels to a proper platter—which will leave their undersides a soggy mess—offer them to guests straight from the fryer via a wire cooling rack. The geometric grid makes for an unexpected visual composition, and nothing else will keep them as beautifully crisp.

CHARRED ENDIVE
WITH WARM GARLIC-CAPER LEMON SAUCE

Grilled endive is unexpected and shockingly delicious; the heat imparts a silky texture and brings out the veggie's natural sugars, tempering its bitterness. This particular preparation is one I keep in my back pocket for early spring, when I'm craving the season's first lettuces but still appreciate some warmth and depth to my meals. It works as a side with fish or meat and feels so sophisticated—though it takes just minutes to achieve those swoony char marks. The real showstopper here is the briny sauce, a mélange of warmed capers, garlic, herbs, and citrus that provides just the right balance to the endive's smoky-sweet bite.

SERVES 4
—

5 tablespoons (75 ml) extra-virgin olive oil, divided

1 small shallot, finely chopped

2 cloves garlic, minced

1 anchovy fillet, minced

2 tablespoons capers, roughly chopped

2 tablespoons fresh lemon juice

1 small handful fresh parsley, finely chopped

4 Belgian endives, halved lengthwise

Salt and freshly cracked pepper

In a saucepan, heat 2 tablespoons of the oil over medium-low heat. Add the shallot and garlic and cook, being careful not to brown them, until the shallot is translucent, 2 to 3 minutes. Add the anchovy and cook for 1 minute. Add the capers and lemon juice and cook until heated through, 1 to 2 minutes.

Transfer the mixture from the saucepan to a small bowl. Stir in the chopped parsley and 2 tablespoons oil. Set aside and keep warm.

Preheat the grill over medium-high heat to about 400°F (205°C). Drizzle the endive with the remaining 1 tablespoon oil and season with salt and pepper. Grill the endive until lightly charred on all sides, 8 to 10 minutes total.

Place the endive on a platter and drizzle with the sauce. Serve with extra sauce on the side.

swoon tip

Larger, sharp-edged pieces of parsley look infinitely more attractive than the usual messy mince. Instead of hacking away at the delicate leaves with your knife, use this pro method that I picked up from Chef Dan Kluger: Bunch the leaves up as tightly as possible on your cutting board and give them a few clean, concise slices.

WHEATBERRY GRAIN BOWL
WITH PICKLED RHUBARB AND HUMBOLDT FOG

Don't tell my friend asparagus, but rhubarb is my favorite of the swoony stalks that pop up each spring. I love the deep pink, bracingly bitter vegetable so much, in fact, that I became hell-bent on figuring out a new way to use her. Instead of sweetening her up as usual, to make a pie or crumble, I amped up her inherent sourness with a quick bath in pickling solution. The tangy result is, I must admit, utterly brilliant—especially when mingled with the creamy goat cheese, snappy raw spring veg, nutty wheatberries, and herby vinaigrette.

SERVES 4 TO 6

—

FOR THE PICKLED RHUBARB

1 cup (240 ml) cider vinegar

1 cup (200 g) sugar

Pinch kosher salt

2 cups (130 g) ½-inch-thick (12-mm-thick) slices rhubarb (about 2 large stalks)

FOR THE VINAIGRETTE

¼ cup (60 ml) champagne vinegar

1 tablespoon honey

1 teaspoon Dijon mustard

½ cup (120 ml) extra-virgin olive oil

2 tablespoons lemon juice

¼ cup (13 g) finely chopped fresh mint

¼ cup (13 g) finely chopped fresh parsley

½ shallot, finely chopped

Salt and freshly cracked pepper

FOR THE WHEATBERRY SALAD

1 cup (185 g) wheatberries

Kosher salt

¾ pound (340 g) snap peas, blanched, shocked

1 head watercress, stalky ends trimmed (or use purple watercress)

3 radishes

2 spring onions, bulbs and light green stems

5 ounces (140 g) Humboldt Fog or other mild goat cheese

Make the pickled rhubarb: Place the cider vinegar, sugar, salt, and 1 cup (240 ml) water in a medium saucepan. Bring to a boil over medium-high heat, stirring until the sugar dissolves. Place the rhubarb in a nonreactive bowl. Slowly pour the hot liquid over the rhubarb and cool to room temperature. Refrigerate until ready to use.

Make the vinaigrette: Whisk together the champagne vinegar, honey, mustard, oil, and lemon juice until well combined. Stir in the mint, parsley, and shallot. Season with salt and pepper.

Make the wheatberry salad: Preheat the oven to 375°F (190°C). Spread the wheatberries evenly on a baking sheet. Bake until the wheatberries are toasted and fragrant, about 10 minutes.

In a medium saucepan, bring 3 cups (720 ml) of heavily salted water to a boil. Add the wheatberries and gently simmer, covered, until tender but chewy, 45 to 60 minutes. Transfer to a large mixing bowl and cool to room temperature. Once the wheatberries have cooled, lightly drizzle them with a small amount of the vinaigrette, reserving the remainder. Stored in an airtight container and refrigerated, the wheatberries can be made and pre-dressed up to 1 week in advance.

While the wheatberries are cooking, prep the remaining ingredients: Thinly slice the snap peas, rinse and dry the watercress, thinly slice the radishes (ideally on a mandoline) and spring onions, and crumble the cheese.

Just before serving, drain the rhubarb. Spoon the wheatberries into a big bowl and top with the rhubarb and vegetables. Pour in about half of the remaining vinaigrette and toss until all the ingredients are evenly coated, adding additional vinaigrette if necessary. Top with crumbled cheese.

When plating a salad with so many different components, layer them to ensure that the prettiest ones are front and center. Here, the rosy rhubarb; vibrant, bias-cut snap peas; and sculptural mint sprigs are added to the bowl on top of the yummy—but less handsome—grains.

GEMELLI WITH ZESTY LEMON, CASTELVETRANO OLIVES, AND PARSLEY

We love big flavors in our family—add some heat, herbs, and mouth-puckering acid to just about anything and you have a meal fit for the Calderones! Case in point: Since the age of four, Jivan has been able make a mean pesto and it's still his favorite sauce for pasta. Yet, I wrestled with whether to include pasta with pesto in this book. If it's simple enough for a preschooler, do we really need a recipe? This dish is my solution. It tips its hat to classic pesto with its herb-based, no-cook sauce, but it's a little less expected, thanks to parsley, olives, hazelnuts, and habaneros.

SERVES 4

—

½ cup (55 g) hazelnuts

Salt and freshly cracked pepper

1 large bunch parsley, minced (about 1¼ cups/65 g)

2 cups (about 10 ounces/280 g) roughly chopped Castelvetrano olives

2 large lemons, grated zest and juice

½ cup (120 ml) extra-virgin olive oil plus 2 tablespoons, plus more for drizzling

Kosher salt

1 pound (455 g) gemelli pasta

3 large cloves garlic

1 to 2 anchovy fillets, depending on your taste

1 cup (100 g) grated ricotta salata, plus shaved ricotta salata for serving

¼ teaspoon minced habanero chile, for serving

Aleppo pepper, for serving

Preheat the oven to 400°F (205°C). Spread the hazelnuts on a baking sheet and toast until lightly golden and fragrant, about 10 minutes.

Place the toasted nuts on a clean dish towel and rub them against one another until they lose most of their skins. Roughly chop the hazelnuts, place them in a bowl, and toss with a generous drizzle of oil. Season with salt and pepper and set aside.

In a medium bowl, mix together the parsley, olives, lemon juice, zest, and ½ cup (120 ml) oil. Set aside.

Bring a large pot of heavily salted water to a boil over medium heat. Add the pasta and cook according to package directions until al dente. Drain, reserving ½ cup (120 ml) of the pasta water.

Mince the garlic and anchovy together until they form almost a paste on your cutting board. In a large skillet, heat the 2 tablespoons oil over medium-high heat until it shimmers. Add the garlic-anchovy paste. Cook, stirring constantly, until the garlic is soft and fragrant, about 1 minute. Reduce the heat to low.

Pour the drained pasta into the skillet. Add the grated cheese and reserved pasta water and toss until the cheese is evenly distributed. Stir in the parsley and olive mixture and toss until the pasta is evenly coated.

Taste and adjust for seasoning and serve topped with toasted hazelnuts, habaneros, shaved cheese, and a sprinkle of Aleppo pepper.

Don't squander the gorgeous green color of Castelvetrano olives by chopping them into unrecognizable bits. Instead, place them on a cutting board and press down on them firmly with the back of a chef's knife. The olives will split, releasing their pits and revealing their roughly torn flesh.

WHOLE STUFFED BRANZINO
WRAPPED IN AN HERB BOUQUET

Cooking a whole fish can be an intimidating prospect, but I promise there's not much to it. For this recipe, the most import-ant thing is to get your hands on pristine, truly fresh branzino. Generally, you'll have the best luck at your local fishmonger rather than the grocery store. (Make a point of befriending him—favorite customers always score the freshest catch.) The skin of the fish should be shiny rather than dull, the eyes clear and not sunken, and the flesh should spring back when you poke it. Have the store clean, scale, and gut the branzino for you—there's no reason to struggle with such messy tasks yourself. Once you get these beauties home, all that's left is to stuff them, after which they can sit patiently in the fridge until you're ready to pop them on the grill or into the oven.

SERVES 4

—

1 large bunch fresh cilantro

1 bunch flowering chives or other flowering herbs such as thyme, cilantro, or lavender

1 large jalapeño, finely chopped (if you're sensitive to heat, remove the seeds)

2 cloves garlic, minced

2 teaspoons minced fresh ginger

2 teaspoons coriander seeds, toasted and crushed

¼ cup (60 ml) extra-virgin olive oil, plus more for drizzling

7 limes, divided

Salt

4 whole branzino (about 1 pound/ 455 g each), scaled and cleaned

Freshly cracked pepper, for serving

Preheat the oven to 400°F (205°C).

Set aside a handful each of cilantro stems and chives for the bouquets, then finely chop the re-mainder; you should end up with about 2 cups (100 g) cilantro and about 3 tablespoons chives. Combine the chopped herbs, jalapeño, garlic, ginger, and coriander. Add the oil, the zest of 1 lime, and 2 tablespoons lime juice. Season to taste with salt.

Line a large baking sheet with parchment paper. Cut eight pieces of kitchen twine. Lay each fish on top of two pieces of twine. Season the cavity of the fish with salt and pepper, then rub with about half of the herb mixture, reserving the remainder. Thinly slice 2 limes and layer them in the cavity of the fish. Drizzle the outside of the fish with oil and season with salt and pepper. Lay a small handful of chive blossoms and cilantro sprigs on top of the fish and tie the twine around it. Make one tie closer to the head, and the other closer to the tail; this will secure the bouquet and help the fish cook evenly. Repeat with each fish and place on the prepared baking sheet. Roast the fish until just opaque throughout when a knife is inserted at the back-bone, 15 to 20 minutes.

While the branzino is roasting, add the juice from 1 lime and a drizzle of oil to the remaining herb mixture. Create a loose sauce, adding more lime juice and oil as needed. Taste and adjust for salt. Cut the remaining limes into wedges.

Serve the branzino on a platter with the lime wedges, a sprinkle of torn chive blossoms, pepper, and the herb sauce on the side.

Channel your inner florist and build an herb bundle like you would a bouquet. Anchor the mix with sturdy sprigs like thyme and oregano, then add flowering varieties like cilantro, chive blossoms, or even lavender.

GRILLED SHRIMP
WITH CHILE, LEMON, AND OREGANO

This is one of those entrées I make on auto-pilot when hosting guests—without fail, it wins over adults and children alike. Simple to prepare, it can easily be doubled or even tripled. That said, there are some things to keep in mind. You can make the marinade in advance, but to ensure that the flavor stays bold, don't add the oregano until the last minute. And don't be tricked into thinking longer is better when marinating. A good rule of thumb for fish or shellfish is ten to fifteen minutes max—any longer and the acids will effectively "cook" the fish. Finally, don't forget to slather on the reserved marinade post-grilling—it's bright, zippy notes really wake up the fire-kissed shrimp.

SERVES 6 AS AN APPETIZER,
OR 4 AS A MAIN COURSE

—

2 pounds (910 g) head-on jumbo
  shrimp, cleaned and deveined

5 medium lemons

8 cloves garlic, chopped

1 teaspoon salt

1 cup (240 ml) extra-virgin olive oil

⅓ cup (10 g) lightly packed fresh
  oregano leaves, finely chopped, plus
  more for garnish

½ teaspoon hot red chile, such as
  Fresno or habanero

Aleppo pepper, for serving

Rinse the shrimp with cold water and pat them dry.

Zest 1 lemon and juice it. Juice another lemon to make ⅓ cup (80 ml) juice total. Cut the remaining   3 lemons into wedges. Set all aside.

In the bowl of a food processor, process the garlic, lemon juice, and salt. With the motor still running, slowly pour in the oil and process until the mixture is smooth and emulsified. Transfer the lemon-garlic sauce to a bowl and stir in the oregano and chile.

Place the shrimp in a bowl and cover with a third of the sauce, reserving the remainder for serving. Marinate for 10 to 15 minutes.

Preheat the grill over medium-high heat to 400°F (205°C). Grill the shrimp until opaque throughout, 3 to 5 minutes per side. Pour the reserved sauce over the shrimp and sprinkle with the oregano, lemon zest, and a pinch of Aleppo pepper. Serve with the lemon wedges.

In appearance as in flavor, this dish is about the shrimp and the sauce—and that's it. So avoid that temptingly convenient mountain of pale, preshelled shrimp at the grocery store and head to your fishmonger for the biggest, reddest, most gorgeous shell-on creatures you can get your hands on. You'll reap the benefits in taste, texture, and natural beauty.

PAN-SEARED SALMON WITH PEAS, CHANTERELLES, AND DILL-CHIVE SAUCE

Admittedly, I was a snob about salmon for years—the ubiquitous fish just seemed so blandly run-of-the-mill. That all changed when I stepped into fashion designer Peter Som's kitchen to shoot a cooking story for EyeSwoon. Peter, who also happens to be an exceptional culinary talent, suggested we make salmon—and I wasn't about to reveal my bias. So we cooked, and I tasted, and you know what? I swooned. Salmon, I realized, is unbelievably supple, flavorful, and rich. And what other protein can boast such a gorgeous hue? Served atop golden chanterelles, vibrant spring peas, and a deep-green herb sauce, this piece of fish is beautifully dressed. Peter would no doubt approve.

SERVES 4

—

FOR THE DILL-CHIVE SAUCE

½ cup (25 g) chopped fresh dill

½ cup (25 g) chopped fresh chives

⅓ cup (70 ml) extra-virgin olive oil

1 clove garlic, finely chopped

Generous pinch salt

1 lemon, grated zest and 1 to 2 tablespoons juice

FOR THE SALMON

4 tablespoons (60 ml) extra-virgin olive oil, divided

1 leek, white and pale green parts only, halved lengthwise and sliced crosswise into ¼-inch (6-mm) half-moons

10 ounces (280 g) chanterelle mushrooms, cleaned and torn, if large

1 cup (145 g) fresh peas, blanched

Salt and freshly cracked pepper

4 (6-ounce/170-g) center-cut, skin-on salmon fillets

1 tablespoon fresh lemon juice

1 handful fresh pea shoots, for garnish

Make the sauce: In the bowl of a food processor, pulse together the dill, chives, oil, garlic, and salt until finely chopped. (You can also do this by hand.) Transfer the mixture to a bowl and set aside.

Make the salmon: In a medium skillet, heat 3 tablespoons of the oil over medium heat. Add the leeks and cook until softened, about 5 minutes, being careful not to brown. Add the chanterelles and cook until tender, about 5 minutes. Add the peas and cook for a few minutes, or just long enough to heat them through. Season with salt and pepper; set aside.

Generously season the salmon fillets on both sides with salt and pepper. In a nonstick skillet, heat the remaining 1 tablespoon oil over medium-high heat. Add the fillets, skin-side down, and sear without disturbing until the skin is golden and crispy, 3 to 4 minutes. Flip and cook until medium-rare, about 3 minutes.

Stir the lemon zest and juice into the sauce, and the tablespoon of lemon juice into the pea mixture. Place the salmon fillets on a bed of the pea mixture and drizzle with dill sauce. Garnish with the pea shoots.

The key to making salmon skin look as good as it tastes is keeping it intact and getting a nice sear on it—both of which are best achieved in a nonstick pan. And wouldn't it be a shame to cover up that crisp, golden gorgeousness? Here, the bright sauce and verdant veggies mingle in the background of the plate, allowing the fish its moment in the spotlight.

YOGURT-MARINATED CHICKEN AND ARTICHOKE SKEWERS WITH HERBED DRESSING

I am curious by nature, so when I first started cooking, I asked a lot of questions. One of my favorites, which I still pose to just about everyone I meet: What is your go-to weeknight meal? In my kitchen, a recipe has to meet certain standards in order to earn that title. I need to be able to prep it ahead, cook it quickly, and serve it straight up—meaning it boasts both veggies and protein. These chicken skewers fit the bill. Juicy grilled chicken is something that eludes even many experienced cooks, but here the yogurt in the marinade tenderizes the meat and prevents it from drying out. I often drizzle these kebabs with lemon-herb vinaigrette and serve tzatziki on the side. Recipes for both can be found in the Sauces and Extras section.

SERVES 6 TO 8

—

FOR THE MARINADE

½ cup (120 ml) plain full-fat Greek yogurt

¼ cup (60 ml) fresh lemon juice (about 2 large lemons)

4 cloves garlic, minced

2½ teaspoons minced fresh ginger

2 tablespoons chopped fresh cilantro

2 tablespoons chopped fresh parsley

¾ cup (180 ml) extra-virgin olive oil

1½ teaspoons Aleppo pepper

2 teaspoons ground cumin

2 teaspoons kosher salt

2 teaspoon smoked paprika

FOR THE SKEWERS

2 pounds (910 g) boneless chicken thigh meat, cut into 2-inch (5-cm) pieces

2 (14-ounce/400-g) cans whole artichoke hearts, drained and halved

2 red onions, cut into 1½-inch (4-cm) pieces

2 small zucchinis, cubed

1 cup cherry tomatoes

Extra-virgin olive oil, for drizzling

Freshly cracked pepper

Lemon-Herb Vinaigrette (page 267), for serving

Tzatziki (page 267), for serving

Make the marinade: In a large bowl, combine all of the ingredients along with the chicken. Stir thoroughly to combine. Cover and refrigerate, allowing the chicken to marinate for a minimum of 3 hours or ideally overnight.

Make the skewers: Drizzle the vegetables with oil and season with salt and pepper. Skewer the chicken, alternating each piece with the vegetables. Discard any extra marinade.

Preheat the grill over medium-high heat to about 400°F (205°C). Grill the skewers until lightly charred and cooked through, about 6 minutes per side. Before serving, drizzle the skewers with the vinaigrette. Serve with the tzatziki and any remaining vinaigrette on the side.

My interior design training taught me that styling just about anything in odd groupings as opposed to even is more visually stimulating—and that's just as true for skewers on a platter as it is for objects on a mantel. (Asymmetry encourages your eye to move around.) Another way to avoid things looking matchy-matchy here: Vary the order of ingredients. Start with a tomato on one skewer, zucchini on the next.

PAN-ROASTED PORK CHOPS WITH SHALLOTS, FENNEL, AND WATERCRESS

I love myself a good pork chop, but that wasn't always the case. When I was a child, the chops that showed up on our dinner table were always dry and tough—yet somehow they maintained their stature as our go-to weeknight meal. It's no surprise, then, that I shied away from cooking them for years. But that all changed when I learned to ignore the myth that pork has to be well done. Now I cook my chops to medium, still slightly pink in the middle. Here, the pork and some veggies get a quick sear in a cast-iron skillet, which is then used to cook up a tangy sauce. It's a truly juicy one-pan wonder.

SERVES 2

—

2 bone-in pork chops, 1- to 1¼-inches (about 2.5 cm) thick, left at room temperature for 30 minutes before cooking

Salt and freshly cracked pepper

1 tablespoon extra-virgin olive oil, plus more for drizzling

4 shallots, peeled and halved lengthwise

1 fennel bulb, quartered and cored, one quarter reserved and the remainder cut into ½-inch-thick (12-mm-thick) wedges, fronds reserved for garnish

4 to 5 sprigs fresh thyme

4 radishes

1 large handful watercress, stalky ends trimmed

1 tablespoon plus ⅓ cup (90 ml) cider vinegar

2 tablespoons whole-grain mustard

2 teaspoons honey

¼ cup (60 ml) chicken stock or water

Flaky sea salt, for serving

Pat the pork dry and season generously with salt and pepper. Preheat a large cast-iron skillet over medium-high heat for 5 minutes. Add the oil and then the pork. Scatter the shallots, fennel wedges, and thyme around the chops. Cook, flipping the pork and tossing the vegetables halfway through, about 8 minutes total. The pork should be cooked through and well browned, and the vegetables should be tender. Using tongs, remove the pork and vegetables to a plate. Cover and keep warm.

While the pork and vegetables are cooking, make the watercress salad: Using a mandoline, thinly shave the radishes and remaining fennel. Toss the shaved vegetables and watercress with 1 tablespoon of the vinegar and a drizzle of oil. Season with salt and pepper. Set aside.

Add the remaining ⅓ cup (75 ml) vinegar to the skillet. Using a rubber or wooden spoon, scrape up any browned bits that are stuck to the bottom of the pan. Stir in the mustard, honey, and ¼ cup (60 ml) water. Simmer until you have a reduced, syrupy sauce. Remove the pan from the heat. Return the pork to the pan and evenly coat with the sauce.

Plate the pork with fennel and shallots and spoon with the pan sauce. Top the pork with a handful of watercress salad. Garnish with the reserved fennel fronds and finish with a pinch of flaky salt.

There are few things less attractive than a pale pork chop. Happily, it's not hard to achieve that deeply golden sear. The key is to get your pan good and hot—and keep it that way. To that end, bring your meat to room temperature before cooking—a cold chop will cool down your pan—and opt for cast iron, which retains heat most evenly.

GINGER-AND-VANILLA-BEAN RHUBARB GALETTE

This is one of those "lemme pat myself on the back" recipes. The first time I tasted it I actually squealed with excitement. The zingy ginger and deeply aromatic flecks of vanilla bean are pretty spectacular, and just the right match for the complex, sour flavor of the rhubarb.

The pastry is also something to swoon over. It's perfectly flaky, which I attribute to a few factors: adding buttermilk to the dough, freezing the butter cubes, and chilling the pastry a second time after it's rolled out. Once you master the method, you'll want to use it again and again—and you can, all year long with just about any fruit that's in season.

SERVES 6

—

FOR THE DOUGH

1½ cups (190 g) all-purpose flour, plus more for work surface

1 tablespoon sugar

½ teaspoon kosher salt

1 stick (½ cup/115g) very cold unsalted butter, cut into small pieces

⅓ cup plus 1 tablespoon (90 ml) very cold buttermilk, well shaken

1 large egg, for brushing the crust

Raw sugar, for sprinkling

FOR THE FILLING

1 pound (455 g) rhubarb, trimmed and cut into 3-inch (7.5-cm) pieces, halved lengthwise if large

¾ cup (150 g) sugar

2 tablespoons all-purpose flour

1 tablespoon fresh lemon juice

1 tablespoon minced fresh ginger

1 vanilla bean, cut lengthwise, seeds scraped and pod reserved for another use (or 3 teaspoons vanilla extract)

Vanilla ice cream, for serving

Make the dough: In a food processor fitted with a metal blade, pulse together the flour, sugar, and salt until combined. Scatter the cubes of butter over the dry ingredients and pulse a few times until the butter is broken up and the mixture resembles a coarse meal. Slowly pour in the buttermilk, pulsing to combine, just until the dough begins to hold together. Transfer the dough to a clean work surface and shape into a square disc. Wrap the dough in plastic and refrigerate for a minimum of 1 hour or up to overnight. The dough can be made up to 2 days in advance and refrigerated.

Preheat the oven to 400°F (205°C).

Line a baking sheet with parchment. On a lightly floured work surface, roll the dough into an approximately 10- by 14-inch (25- by 35-cm) rectangle. Carefully transfer to the baking sheet and refrigerate briefly while you prepare the filling.

Make the filling: In a large bowl, toss all of the ingredients together until well combined. Use your fingers to break up any clumps of vanilla seeds; they should be distributed evenly throughout the filling.

Pour the filling onto the center of the dough, leaving a 2- to 3-inch (5- to 7.5-cm) border along the edges. Fold the edges up over the filling and press gently to seal.

Make an egg wash by whisking the egg with 1 tablespoon water. Brush the dough with the egg wash and sprinkle with raw sugar. Bake until the crust is golden and the fruit is bubbling, 30 to 35 minutes. Transfer to a wire rack and cool slightly before serving with a scoop of vanilla ice cream.

Presentation rule of thumb—embrace imperfections. If your scoop of ice cream starts to melt all over your pastry, all the better! There is nothing quite as enticing as a gooey galette, and there is beauty in letting ingredients do what they do naturally.

CHERRY AND APRICOT POLENTA CRISP

Even if you're not an expert baker, this is a dessert you can count on—and it's great for entertaining since it can be made in advance. What sets it apart is the addition of polenta, or Italian cornmeal, to the topping; it lends a deliciously granular crunch. And it's highly adaptable, too. Apricots and cherries are my favorite late-spring combination (word to the wise: Invest in a cherry pitter), but the dish works with almost any fruit that's in season. And you could easily sub vanilla ice cream for the crème fraîche. No surprise, it's become a year-round staple in my dessert repertoire.

SERVES 6 TO 8

—

¾ cup (95 g) all-purpose flour

⅔ cup (120 g) quick-cooking polenta

⅓ cup (75 g) packed light brown sugar

1 teaspoon baking powder

¾ teaspoon salt

10 tablespoons (140 g) unsalted butter, cut into pieces, at room temperature

1 large egg

1½ pounds (680 g) apricots, cut into 1-inch (2.5-cm) wedges

1½ pounds (680 g) sweet cherries, pitted

1 lemon, grated zest and juice

⅓ cup (65 g) granulated sugar

4 teaspoons cornstarch

Crème fraîche, for serving

Preheat the oven to 375°F (190°C).

In a medium bowl, stir together the flour, polenta, light brown sugar, baking powder, and salt. Using your fingers, work the butter into the mixture until it resembles coarse meal. Stir in the egg until well combined.

In a 2-quart baking dish (about 9 by 13 inches/23 by 33 cm), toss together the apricots, cherries, lemon zest and juice, granulated sugar, and cornstarch. Clump the crumble topping together as you scatter it over the fruit.

Bake the crisp until the fruit is bubbling and the topping is golden brown, about 35 minutes. Cool slightly before serving. Serve with a dollop of crème fraîche.

swoon tip

As you scatter on the crumble topping, be sure to allow areas of fruit to peek out. The exposed cherries and apricots will bubble over beautifully when baked, offering a colorful teaser of what lies beneath.

YOGURT PANNA COTTA
WITH STRAWBERRIES AND SABA

I was eighteen and on my first trip to Italy, with my mother and aunt, when I first encountered the creamy, wiggly-wobbly goodness known as panna cotta. It was hands down the best sweet I had ever tasted but, somehow, once I returned home, I forgot its name. For years my mom and I reminisced longingly about this mysterious Italian treat, until about a decade later when I finally tasted it again at one of my favorite Brooklyn eateries. I actually called my mom from the table screaming, "PANNA COTTA, PANNA COTTA!" We had a good laugh and since then I have made it for many family gatherings. This version is my go-to. The slight tang of the Greek yogurt sets the custard apart and the saba, a sweet grape vinegar, cuts through the richness. (If you can't find saba, just simmer balsamic vinegar until it's reduced by half.) In peak season I love to serve my panna cotta with fresh strawberries; it feels like an update on classic strawberries with cream. The rest of the year, macerate the berries to deepen their flavor. See page 266 for my recipe.

SERVES 6

—

2 teaspoons powdered, unflavored gelatin

2 cups (480 ml) heavy cream

7 tablespoons (about 90 g) sugar

1 vanilla bean, halved lengthwise, seeds scraped

⅛ teaspoon kosher salt

1 cup (240 ml) full-fat Greek yogurt

1 pint (340 g) strawberries, trimmed and halved, quartered if large

Saba or syrupy balsamic vinegar, for drizzling

In a small bowl, sprinkle the gelatin over 2 tablespoons water and let stand to soften and dissolve. In a medium saucepan, combine the cream, sugar, vanilla bean and seeds, and salt. Bring to a simmer over medium heat, then remove the saucepan from heat. Stir in the gelatin until fully dissolved. Add the yogurt, whisking gently until combined. Divide the mixture between six ramekins and cool to room temperature. Cover the ramekins with plastic wrap and refrigerate for at least 3 hours or up to 2 days. (You can also expedite the setting process by popping the ramekins in the freezer for 15 to 20 minutes.)

Just before serving, run a sharp knife around the edge of each ramekin and dip the ramekin base in a hot water bath for about 10 seconds. Invert the panna cottas onto individual plates. Serve garnished with strawberries and drizzled with saba.

 The beauty of panna cotta lies in its pristine, gleaming white surface. To keep the custard intact, remove these suckers from their vessels with care. Use your thinnest, most flexible knife to separate the panna cotta from the edges of the ramekin and shake ever so gently to unmold.

THE

SPRING

TABLE

Spring is all about clean, fresh flavors, so it's only fitting to echo that lovely sense of lightness and simplicity in the décor. Here, in lieu of fancy flowers, the season's verdant vines and veggies beautify the table, with crisp linens and subtly textured dinner plates—all of them in shades of white—serving as a serene, elegant backdrop. Warming things up are purple artichokes, blush glassware and rose-gold flatware, which highlight the subtle hints of pink in the gorgeously fresh food. Sometimes less is truly more.

No. 1
ON THE ROCKS

Spring's swoony beauty can, in fact, be frozen in time. Edible flowers and herbs, preserved in cubes of ice, are the prettiest additions to just about any spring cocktail.

No. 2
THE DIVINE VINE

Sometimes the best vase is no vase at all. Here, I laid delicate spring-y vines directly on the white linen tablecloth, weaving their leaves and tendrils between a row of simple, hand-glazed candlesticks.

No. 3
PLANT YOUR PLACE

This time of year, when herbs and microgreens are so abundant, it seems only natural to include them on the table, as well as in the food. Dainty ceramic pots planted with delicate sprouts serve as chic place card holders and thoughtful parting gifts.

No. 4
HIGH CONTRAST

One design rule you don't want to break: Opposites attract. The tough spikes of baby purple artichokes are balanced by sweet and delicate dill blossoms. With produce this pretty, who needs flowers?

No. 5
SOUR POWER

With their gorgeous hue and extremely short season, chive blossoms are highly coveted in spring. Extend their ephemeral beauty by using them to infuse vinegar—and share the wealth by sending jars home with your guests.

No. 6
CARRY ON

Tote your nibbles wherever spring might take you. One of the chicest ways to transport your picnic provisions is also one of the simplest: Wrap mason jars in simple rustic linen or burlap, tying the cloth in a loose knot to create a handle.

No. 7
NATURAL RESOURCES

Inspiration can strike in the most unexpected places—in this case, at the garden center. While at the nursery to stock my herb garden, I came across these young broccoli plants. Simply potted and wrapped with cheesecloth and cooking twine, they serve as gorgeously sculptural table décor.

No. 8
VERDANT VARIETY

To keep a monochromatic palette from looking one-note, play with tone and texture. Here, varying shades of green adds visual depth to a place setting, as does the juxtaposition of rough, nubby linen and smooth ceramic.

No. 9
THAT'S A WRAP

Even disposable cutlery can have style. Compared to plastic, bamboo flatware is easier on the environment, and on the eyes—especially when bundled with a linen napkin and tied with color-coordinated twine.

SUMMER

THE MOMENT SCHOOL GETS OUT, my family and I move full-time to Amagansett, to a little bayside hamlet called Barnes Landing. Having previously lived year-round in New York City, buying our house on the East End of Long Island has brought about a dramatic shift in our lives.

Whereas the rest of the year we hop on the subway, hustling from Brooklyn to Manhattan, during summer we take bike rides through our quiet town, stopping to hunt for clams and build forts out of sun-drenched driftwood. We've discovered surfing—particularly my son, who has embraced both the sport and its community. Our days are long and languid, often spent on the beach with friends, from morning until sunset.

Besides deepening my family's relationship to nature and to one another, spending time in Amagansett has also changed the way I approach summer cooking. Every aspect of the process just seems to relax and take on the arms-wide-open quality of my surroundings.

Perhaps the most significant change has stemmed from my discovery of the local farms. Their vibrant seasonal produce has lent new excitement to my kitchen. I adore the intimate, small-town approach to buying provisions, driving from place to place to gather my treasures. I head to Stuart's, our local fishmonger, for the catch of the day; cruise by Balsam Farms to scoop up corn and tomatoes; and stop by Vicki's Veggies (daily!) to snag a loaf of their cult-classic zucchini bread. The best discovery has been my neighbor Todd's just-laid eggs with their eye-popping orange yolks! Purchasing on the honor system, I just grab a dozen and leave five dollars in the cooler.

If you hunt down the very best ingredients, all you really need to do is let them shine. And that's what I love most about summer cooking: Because it's less about technique, you can be a bit more spontaneous. No one expects a fancy reduction over a beautifully grilled fish. You can loosen the reins and embrace what's in front of you.

Once I've gathered up the produce, I gather family and friends to fill our home. These months are all about sandy feet, a revolving door of guests, children on the zipline or splashing in the pool (we've coined our house "Camp Calderone"), and all hands on deck in the kitchen, preparing an impromptu family-style feast.

Whether we're making grilled fish, summer squash salad, or a thick-cut rib-eye, charred to perfection, the approach is always the same: Keep it simple. This is food that asks only for a squeeze of lemon, a shower of herbs, and a dusting of sea salt. It's devoured during a laid-back dinner on the lawn—or even better, the beach. Summer is the season for carefree meals. So, dig in—you have permission to play!

IN SEASON

BASIL

BLUEBERRIES

CILANTRO

CORN

CUCUMBERS

EGGPLANT

GREEN BEANS

MELONS

NECTARINES

PARSLEY

PEACHES

PEPPERS

PLUMS

RASPBERRIES

SUMMER SQUASH

TOMATILLOS

TOMATOES

A DUO OF SUMMER CROSTINI

Crostini are an infinitely adaptable way to whip up something delicious from whatever I happen to have on hand. In this case, I used blueberries from the farm stand, bright pink radishes courtesy of my CSA box, fresh ricotta from the Italian market, and some fragrant herbs snipped from my garden, but think of the recipe as a loose blueprint to use with any seasonal fruits and veggies. Figs or pears would be lovely with the ricotta, for instance, while cucumbers or cherries would pair deliciously with the goat cheese. Once united with a perfectly golden and crunchy little toast, these seemingly disparate elements make for the yummiest of snacks.

SERVES 4 TO 6

—

FOR THE BLUEBERRY CROSTINI

1 small baguette, sliced on the bias
  into ½-inch (12-mm) slices

Extra-virgin olive oil, for drizzling

1 cup (240 ml) fresh ricotta, the best
  you can find

½ cup (75 g) fresh blueberries

2 to 3 sprigs fresh thyme, leaves
  removed

Wildflower honey, for drizzling

1 lemon

Flaky sea salt

FOR THE RADISH CROSTINI

1 small baguette, sliced on the bias
  into ½-inch (12-mm) slices

Extra-virgin olive oil, for drizzling

4 ounces (115 g) fresh goat cheese

4 radishes, thinly sliced

½ lemon, juiced

Salt and freshly cracked pepper

4 to 5 sprigs fresh green herbs such as
  dill, tarragon, or chives, chopped

Microgreens, for garnish (optional)

Flaky sea salt and freshly cracked
  pepper, for serving

Make the blueberry crostini: Preheat the broiler. Place the baguette slices on a baking sheet and drizzle both sides lightly with oil. Broil until golden, 1 to 2 minutes per side, depending on the strength of your broiler. Once the toast has cooled, top each slice with about 1 tablespoon cheese. Arrange some blueberries on top, then sprinkle with thyme leaves and drizzle with honey. Zest the lemon over the crostini. Finish with a sprinkle of flaky sea salt.

Make the radish crostini: Preheat the broiler. Place the baguette slices on a baking sheet and drizzle both sides lightly with oil. Broil until golden, 1 to 2 minute per side, depending on the strength of your broiler. Once the toast has cooled, spread each slice with 1 to 2 tablespoons cheese. In a small bowl, toss the radishes with the lemon juice and a drizzle of oil. Season with salt and pepper. Divide the mixture among the crostini. Scatter with herbs and microgreens, if using, and finish with a sprinkle of flaky sea salt and a few twists of pepper.

 swoon tip

When cutting your radishes, don't be afraid to mix things up. Shaving some into rounds, others vertically or on the bias, makes for a much more interesting composition. No matter the shape, the secret to keeping the slices crisp—and getting those swoony curled edges—is giving them a quick bath in ice water.

STRAWBERRY AND SUN GOLD TOMATO SALAD WITH HONEY-LIME CITRONETTE

This recipe was inspired by one I savored many times while Dan Kluger was the chef at ABC Kitchen in Manhattan. The contrast between the crunchy cucumber, sweet delicate strawberries, and creamy goat cheese is just spectacular—straight up summer on a plate. Tarragon lends an unexpected, anise-like note, while the honey-sweetened lime citronette brings everything together with a zippy, refreshing punch. The dressing is also versatile enough to be used on almost any salad, which is fortunate, because you'll want to make it again and again. For the best flavor, look for tiny Tristar strawberries at the farmer's market. If you can't find them, regular strawberries will do. Just half or quarter them.

SERVES 4 TO 6

—

FOR THE CITRONETTE

3 or 4 limes, 1 zested, all juiced to make ⅓ cup (75 ml)

1 tablespoon honey

¼ cup (60 ml) fruity extra-virgin olive oil

¼ cup (60 ml) grapeseed oil

Salt and freshly cracked pepper

FOR THE SALAD

4 mini seedless cucumbers, cut into ½-inch (12-mm) rounds (about 12 ounces/340 g total)

12 ounces (340 g) mini strawberries, trimmed

1 pint (10 to 12 ounces/280 to 340 g) Sun Gold cherry tomatoes, halved

½ teaspoon finely diced serrano chile

1 small bunch fresh mint, chopped, a handful reserved for garnish

1 small bunch fresh tarragon, chopped, a handful reserved for garnish

⅓ cup (40 g) crumbled soft goat cheese

Flaky sea salt and freshly cracked pepper, for serving

Make the citronette: In a small bowl, whisk together the lime zest, juice, and honey. Slowly whisk in the oils. Season with salt and pepper.

Make the salad: Place the cucumbers, strawberries, tomatoes, and chile in a large bowl. Lightly drizzle with about half of the dressing and toss to coat. Add additional dressing as needed. Sprinkle with the chopped herbs and toss to combine.

To serve, top with the cheese and sprinkle with the reserved herbs, flaky sea salt, and freshly cracked pepper.

Be sure to add the goat cheese at the very end so that it doesn't get mushy and muddle the salad's other colorful components. To keep the veggies from wilting, add the dressing and salt just before serving.

SUMMER SQUASH SALAD
WITH ARUGULA AND FETA

It's sweltering outside, you've been running around all day, and now you just need a refreshing dish you can throw together in a flash. That's where this salad comes in. Not only is it my no-cook solution for hot, busy nights, it also happens to be one of my favorite ways to showcase summer squash. Here, the star veggie is served raw, sliced into skinny strips, and paired with peppery arugula and salty feta cheese. And that hint of unexpected flavor? That's thanks to the dressing, which uses every part of the lemon except the seeds. The combination of rind and pith lends a mild, pleasing bitterness, making this salad not quite as simple as it seems.

SERVES 4
—

FOR THE DRESSING

½ lemon, seeded, sliced into ⅛-inch-
thick (3-mm-thick) rounds, and finely
chopped

2 tablespoons fresh lemon juice

1 teaspoon honey

1 clove garlic, minced

½ shallot or 2 green onions, finely
chopped

¼ cup (60 ml) extra-virgin olive oil

Salt and freshly cracked pepper

FOR THE SALAD

1 medium yellow summer squash

1 medium zucchini

2 cups (40 g) lightly packed baby
arugula

½ cup (25 g) lightly packed fresh
mint, leaves roughly torn

½ cup (20 g) lightly packed fresh
basil, leaves roughly torn

4 ounces (115 g) Bulgarian feta
cheese, thinly sliced

¼ cup (35 g) toasted hazelnuts, skins
removed (see page 46 for method)

Flaky sea salt and freshly cracked
pepper, for serving

Make the dressing: In a small bowl, whisk together the chopped lemon, lemon juice, honey, garlic, shallot, and oil. Season with salt and pepper.

Make the salad: Using a mandoline, spiralizer, or sharp knife, julienne the squash and zucchini and place them in a large bowl with the arugula, mint, and basil. Drizzle with the dressing and toss until all of the ingredients are evenly coated.

To serve, transfer the salad to a deep serving bowl and scatter it with the feta and hazelnuts. Sprinkle with flaky sea salt and freshly cracked pepper. Serve at room temperature.

swoon tip

The key to a stunning presentation here is using your mandoline's julienne blade to turn out beautifully precise little ribbons of squash. To avoid slicing your fingers into ribbons in the process, hold your veggie with a kitchen towel as you apply downward pressure, using the towel as a barrier between the sharp blade and your skin. Be sure to discard the seedy middle of the squash, which is watery and devoid of color.

PEACHES AND BURRATA
WITH PICKLED SHALLOT

I spend summer in a sweet, peachy haze. These super-juicy suckers without doubt have a hold on me. Ridiculously aromatic and so tender at the height of the season, the fruit is almost seductive. This modern Caprese salad is a love letter to those golden jewels. In this dish, sweet and tangy pickled shallots mingle with ripe peaches and burrata, the creamiest cheese known to man. The result is intensely satisfying and super simple to throw together!

A note on the herbs: I used purple opal basil, as it was abundant at the farm stand and so visually arresting, but it is certainly not essential to the dish. Standard green basil will offer the same herbaceous flavor.

SERVES 4

—

8 ounces (225 g) burrata

2 ripe peaches, halved and thinly sliced

1 cup (40 g) torn fresh basil, both green and purple, if you can find it

¼ cup (25 grams) Pickled Shallots (page 268), plus 1 to 2 tablespoons of pickling liquid

2 tablespoons extra-virgin olive oil

Flaky sea salt and freshly cracked pepper, for serving

1 lime

Roughly tear the burrata, pulling it apart at the center, and arrange it on a plate. Top it with the peaches, basil, and pickled shallots. Drizzle with the oil and pickling liquid. Season with flaky sea salt and pepper and finish by zesting the lime directly over the salad.

This salad is the best kind of artful mess, but there is a method to making it look perfectly imperfect. Start with an oval or rectangular plate large enough to allow negative space on all sides. Turn it vertically and anchor the dish with mounds of burrata at the top and bottom, then arrange the peaches in a loose "s" shape, topping them with a disorderly smattering of shallots and herbs.

HONEYDEW, FENNEL, AND CAPER BERRY SALAD

In high summer, melons are amazingly sweet and refreshing—so why reserve them for snacks? To lend the fruit some savory glory, I used one of my favorite tricks: pickling. It does such sublime things to ingredients like honeydew. And the cooling fennel here helps beat the heat of the serrano, while also offering a fresh crunch. The final surprise: caper berries, which add a uniquely briny touch. To ensure your melon is ripe, follow your nose: The fruit should smell sweet and slightly floral.

SERVES 4 TO 6

—

FOR THE SALAD

½ ripe honeydew melon, seeds removed

1 small fennel bulb, trimmed, halved, and thinly sliced on a mandoline, fronds reserved for garnish

6 to 8 caper berries, halved lengthwise

1 serrano chile, thinly sliced into rounds

FOR THE DRESSING

¼ cup (25 grams) Pickled Shallots (page 268), plus 2 tablespoons of pickling liquid

¼ cup (60 ml) extra-virgin olive oil

1 tablespoon chopped fresh mint, plus a handful of leaves for garnish

Flaky sea salt and freshly cracked pepper, for serving

Make the salad: Cut the honeydew into ½-inch-thick (12-mm-thick) half-moons and remove the peel. Place the melon on a serving platter or in a shallow serving bowl. Add the sliced fennel, caper berries, and chile. Scatter the pickled shallots over the salad.

Make the dressing: Whisk the pickling liquid with the oil. Stir in the chopped mint. Pour the dressing over the salad, tossing until it's evenly coated. Garnish with the reserved mint leaves and fennel fronds. Season with flaky sea salt and freshly cracked pepper.

The pale pastel palette of this dish finds its counterpoint in dark, ragged chunks of freshly cracked pepper. To get them, steer clear of your pepper grinder. Instead, gently crush the peppercorns with the underside of a pan, repeating the process until you get a rough, grainy consistency.

QUINOA TABBOULEH
WITH NECTARINES AND HEIRLOOM TOMATOES

As you've likely noticed by now, I'm a sweet and savory gal. One of my favorite ways to play with that dichotomy is by adding fruit to my salads. In high summer, there's no better combination than nectarines and heirloom tomatoes. The two are such a good match, in fact, that I've been making a version of this salad regularly for years. When sprinkled with a little salt, the nectarines take on a whole new identity—one that perfectly complements the acidity of the tomatoes, the sting of the habaneros, and vibrant flavor of the herbs.

SERVES 4 TO 6

—

FOR THE DRESSING

2 cloves garlic, minced

1 lemon, zested and juiced

1 teaspoon minced habanero chile

3 tablespoons red wine vinegar

½ cup (120 ml) extra-virgin olive oil

Flaky sea salt and freshly cracked
   pepper

FOR THE SALAD

¾ cup (130 g) quinoa

2 pounds (910 g) mixed heirloom
   tomatoes, cut into wedges

½ red onion, thinly sliced

2 nectarines, cut into wedges

1 small bunch fresh basil, torn, a
   handful reserved for garnish (see
   Swoon Tip)

1 small bunch fresh mint, torn, a
   handful reserved for garnish

1 small bunch fresh parsley, torn, a
   handful reserved for garnish

Flaky sea salt, for serving

Make the dressing: Whisk together the garlic, lemon juice and zest, chile, and vinegar. Slowly whisk in the oil. Season with salt and pepper.

Make the salad: Cook the quinoa according to the package directions. Drain and allow it to cool.

In a medium bowl, toss the tomatoes with the onions and just enough dressing to coat. Allow them to sit for a few moments to release some of the juices. Gently toss in the quinoa, nectarines, and herbs. Add more dressing as needed. Just before serving, garnish with the reserved herbs and a sprinkle of flaky sea salt.

Rather than chopping your herbs, treat them as you would any other salad green. Roughly torn mint, basil, and parsley leaves add pops of color to the tone-on-tone nectarines and tomatoes. While prepping them, put a few unplucked sprigs aside for garnish. Their wild and wispy contours offer great visual texture.

CHARRED AND RAW CORN SALAD
WITH TOMATILLO RELISH

Prepping corn is one of my favorite ways to get everyone involved with cooking: My yard is often filled with kids shucking poolside as reggae blasts from speakers on the deck. In Amagansett, we buy ours by the bushel from Balsam Farms. It never needs butter or salt, and we often eat it raw or charred on the grill. This salad lets you have it both ways.

The recipe came about almost by accident. I was making tomatillo salsa and had no idea that tomatillos are supposed to be roasted first. I chopped them up raw and let them macerate in vinegar with some scallions—and I was blown away by the delicious result. I tossed the salsa with some corn as a little taste test, and just like that, a salad was born!

SERVES 6 TO 8
—

FOR THE RELISH

2 tablespoons fresh lime juice

2 tablespoons champagne vinegar

⅓ cup (75 ml) extra-virgin olive oil

2 cloves garlic, minced

2 tablespoons honey

2 teaspoons kosher salt

8 green onions, white and light green parts only, finely diced

½ teaspoon minced habanero chile

12 ounces (340 g) tomatillos, husks removed, finely diced

FOR THE SALAD

6 ears corn, husks and silks removed

Olive oil

4 radishes, cut into thin matchsticks

1 jalapeño, sliced into thin rounds

2 to 3 ounces (55 to 85 g) crumbled feta cheese

Small handful of torn fresh herbs, like cilantro and dill

1 lime, zested and juiced

Make the relish: In a large bowl, whisk together the lime juice, vinegar, oil, garlic, honey, and salt until well combined. Add the onions, habanero, and tomatillos to the mixture and toss to coat. Set aside to macerate at room temperature for 1 to 2 hours.

Make the salad: Preheat a grill over medium-high to 400°F (205°C) or set a grill pan on the stove over high heat. Rub four ears of corn with oil until they are evenly coated. Put the ears of corn on the grill and cook until char marks appear on the kernels, about 4 minutes per side. Remove the corn from the grill and set it aside until it's cool enough to be handled comfortably. Using a sharp knife, cut the kernels off both the charred and remaining two raw cobs directly into a large bowl. Add the radishes and jalapeño and toss to mix until combined.

After macerating for 1 to 2 hours, the tomatillo relish will have accumulated about ¼ to ½ cup (60 to 120 ml) of liquid. Pour off half of this liquid (you can either discard or reserve it to dress another salad—it's delicious!). Pour the tomatillo relish over the corn and mix to combine. You can let the salad sit, covered, at room temperature for up to overnight; before serving, top it with the cheese, torn herbs, and lime zest and juice.

This salad is all about embracing juxtaposition. Because the ingredients are sliced into different shapes, the radish matchsticks provide geometric contrast to the jalapeño rounds. And the corn is the true workhorse: Served raw, charred, in kernels, and in clusters, it's proof a single vegetable can provide a range of flavors, temperatures, and textures. As you slice it off the cob, be sure to keep some larger chunks intact for maximum variety.

CHARRED EGGPLANT
WITH ZA'ATAR AND YOGURT TAHINI

Eggplant on the grill is a favorite in our household. Its firm skin protects its creamy interior but practically melts away in the heat of the fire. These veggies absorb just about anything they come in contact with, making them a great vehicle for a variety of flavors. Here za'atar, a thyme- and sesame-based Middle Eastern spice blend, lends the vegetable both tangy and aromatic notes. The yogurt-tahini sauce, meanwhile, provides deeply nutty and cooling accents. Finally, sumac, a lemony herb that's also a mainstay of Middle Eastern cuisine, brightens the dish with a hit of acid. And if you feel like switching things up—or have a glut of squash in your garden—this recipe can also be prepared with zucchini in place of eggplant.

SERVES 4 TO 6
—

3 Italian eggplants (about 1¾ pounds/800 g total), quartered lengthwise

⅓ cup (75 ml) extra-virgin olive oil

1 tablespoon za'atar, plus more for sprinkling

Salt and freshly cracked pepper

1 lemon, zested and juiced

Yogurt-Tahini Sauce (page 268), for serving

1 handful torn fresh herbs such as parsley, mint, and dill, for serving

Ground sumac, for garnish

Warm flatbread (page 270), for serving

Preheat the grill over medium-high heat to about 400°F (205°C).

Drizzle the oil evenly over the eggplant and toss to coat. Sprinkle it with za'atar and season with salt and pepper. Rub the seasonings into the eggplant, being careful to coat the pieces evenly.

Grill the eggplant on each cut side for 5 to 7 minutes. Turn it skin-side down and grill for 2 minutes more, or until the eggplant has nice grill marks and is tender throughout.

Transfer the eggplant to a platter and drizzle it with the lemon juice, zest, and some of the tahini sauce. Scatter with the fresh herbs and sprinkle with sumac and more za'atar. Serve with warm flatbread and extra tahini sauce on the side.

Achieving the effortless-looking cascade of yogurt-tahini sauce atop this eggplant does, in fact, require some effort. Rather than pouring the sauce directly onto the dish, use a spoon to drizzle it delicately, on the diagonal. Thin the mixture out with a few spoonfuls of warm water if it's too thick to drizzle.

MUSTARDY SMASHED NEW POTATOES WITH JALAPEÑO GREMOLATA

These little gems are about to become your next big summer romance; they've certainly inspired their share of love affairs around my table. Creamy on the inside, crisp and almost caramelized on the outside, they're tossed with grainy mustard and topped with a jalapeño gremolata that lends them an aromatic blast of heat. The combination is so irresistible that you won't think twice about stepping away from the grill to turn on the oven in the middle of summer. And anyway, who doesn't want potatoes with their grilled steak?

SERVES 4 TO 6

—

2 pounds (910 g) baby new potatoes

3 tablespoons olive oil, plus more for drizzling

Salt and freshly cracked pepper

Small handful fresh parsley, roughly chopped

Small handful fresh dill, roughly chopped

2 jalapeños, 1 seeded and finely diced, 1 sliced into rounds

1 small clove garlic, minced

1 lemon

2 tablespoons whole-grain mustard

Flaky sea salt, for serving

Preheat the oven to 425°F (220°C).

Bring a large pot of salted water to a boil. Add the potatoes and simmer until they're tender, 10 to 15 minutes, depending on the size of your potatoes. Drain in a colander. Using a flat-bottomed cup or mug, gently smash the potatoes. Turn them onto a baking sheet; use two sheets if necessary to avoid overcrowding. Drizzle the potatoes generously with some oil and season with salt and pepper. Roast until they're golden, about 15 minutes, then flip and roast until golden and crispy all over, about 10 minutes more.

In a small bowl, mix together the parsley, dill, diced jalapeño, and garlic. Zest half of the lemon over the mixture, add the oil, and toss to combine. Season with salt and pepper.

Toss the roasted potatoes with the mustard, then arrange them on a platter. Spoon the gremolata over the potatoes and scatter them with the jalapeño rounds. Zest the remaining lemon half over the platter. Drizzle the potatoes with the juice from one lemon half. Sprinkle with flaky sea salt and serve immediately.

Crispy spuds not only taste better, they look beautiful, too, with their deep golden hue and lacy, caramelized edges. The key to pretty potatoes: Get them good and dry. After boiling, drain them and then return them to the pot for 2 minutes over super-low heat to burn off any residual moisture.

BUCATINI WITH SPICY SUMMER TOMATOES

There's a good reason why there's only one pasta recipe in this chapter: It's the one that I turn to again and again, all summer long. At the heart of this dish are cherry tomatoes, those stars of late summer. While all tomatoes have a place in my kitchen, I'm particularly enamored of these little jewels for their sweet, nuanced flavor. Cooked until they just burst open, they're then infused with a touch of fresh chile and a bright punch of lemon.

Because this recipe is so simple, salt and pasta water are very much your friends here. Salting early and often helps break down the tomatoes, which enhances their flavor and helps release their sweet juices. Saving the pasta water is also crucial. Its starch, coupled with the pecorino's richness, binds and thickens the dish, melding all of the ingredients.

SERVES 6

—

⅓ cup (75 ml) extra-virgin olive oil, plus more for drizzling

5 cloves garlic, smashed and sliced

3 pints (30 to 36 ounces/850 to 1,020 g) cherry tomatoes, 1 pint halved

1 teaspoon finely diced habanero chile

Salt and freshly cracked pepper

2 lemons, zested and juiced

1 pound (455 g) dried bucatini

⅓ cup (35 g) grated pecorino, plus more for serving

1 cup (40 g) lightly packed fresh basil, roughly chopped, plus more for serving

1 cup (50 g) lightly packed fresh parsley, roughly chopped, plus more for serving

Heat the oil in a large saucepan over medium heat. Add the garlic and cook until it is light golden, about 2 minutes. Add all of the tomatoes and chile. Season generously with salt. Cook until the tomatoes begin to burst, 8 to 10 minutes. Stir in half the lemon zest and all the lemon juice. Continue to cook until most of the tomatoes have burst and begun to break down, 3 to 5 minutes. Set them aside and cover to keep warm.

Bring a large pot of salted water to a boil. Add the bucatini and cook according to the package directions until al dente.

Reserve 1 cup (240 ml) of the pasta water, then drain the pasta and return it to the pot. Add the tomato mixture, pecorino, and ½ cup (120 ml) of the pasta water to the pot and toss to combine. Add additional pasta water, as needed, to make a light sauce. Stir in the fresh herbs and a generous drizzle of olive oil. Season with salt and pepper.

To serve, sprinkle the pasta with additional herbs, pepper, pecorino, and the remaining lemon zest.

swoon tip

It can be tempting to heap pasta into one massive dish, nonna style, but I find that piling it into individual shallow, wide-rim bowls elevates its visual impact. The key is to use a pair of tongs. As you place the bucatini in the bowl, gently grab some noodles and give them a twist so they turn in on themselves. You want to create a loose nest, making sure a few tomatoes and herbs are able to peek through.

FISH TACOS WITH PICKLED CABBAGE
AND PINEAPPLE SALSA

Digging in to fish tacos always takes me back to the very first time I made them. It was my first season on Long Island's East End and I was discovering a whole new landscape and meeting new friends. On a sunny afternoon, a group of us piled into the kitchen, armed with a fish taco recipe we'd found in the *New York Times*. One friend prepped the cabbage, another diced the tomatoes, and I whipped up the black beans. As we chopped and chatted, I remember feeling it was the beginning of something special. Even though I hadn't spent much time in this unfamiliar place, I was already feeling at home.

SERVES 4

—

FOR THE CABBAGE

3 cups (285 g) shredded green
  cabbage
2 jalapeños, cut into thin rounds
1½ cups (360 ml) white wine vinegar
¼ cup (50 g) sugar
2 teaspoons kosher salt
1 teaspoon black peppercorns
1 teaspoon coriander seeds

FOR THE FLOUNDER

2 pounds (910 g) flounder or fluke
  fillets (any delicate white fish will do)
3 tablespoons finely chopped red
  onion
¼ teaspoon minced habanero chile
1 teaspoon ground cumin
½ orange, zested and juiced
A few sprigs fresh cilantro, chopped
2 tablespoons extra-virgin olive oil,
  plus more for the grill
Salt and freshly cracked pepper
3 limes, thinly sliced, for grilling
  (optional)

FOR SERVING

Corn tortillas
Pineapple Salsa (page 271)
Avocado Cream (page 268)
1 or 2 radishes, thinly sliced
A few sprigs fresh cilantro
Lime wedges

Make the cabbage: In a large bowl, combine the cabbage and jalapeños. In a small pot, bring the vinegar, 1 cup (240 ml) water, the sugar, salt, peppercorns, and coriander seeds to a boil. Stir until the sugar and salt have fully dissolved. Pour over the cabbage and jalapeños. Let them cool to room temperature, then drain them in a colander. Put the pickled cabbage into a bowl and set it aside; refrigerated, it will keep for up to 1 day.

Make the flounder: Preheat the grill over medium-high heat to about 400°F (205°C). Place the fish in a baking dish. In a small bowl, mix together all of the marinade ingredients. Pour the marinade over the flounder and let it sit for at least 10 but no more than 20 minutes. Remove the fish from the marinade and drain off the excess.

Grill the tortillas until they're lightly charred. Wrap them in aluminum foil and put them on the cooler part of the grill to keep them warm (when you're ready to serve them, wrap them in a kitchen towel to keep them from drying out). Oil the grill grates well and grill the fish until it's cooked through and lightly charred, 1½ to 2 minutes per side.

Alternatively, to avoid sticking, you can grill the fish on a bed of sliced limes until it turns opaque and is cooked through, about 3 minutes total; if you use this method, there's no need to flip the fish.

Just before serving, use your fingers to tear the fish into chunky pieces. Serve it immediately on the warm tortillas topped with pickled cabbage, pineapple salsa, avocado cream, sliced radishes, and torn cilantro. Serve the limes wedges on the side.

Tacos have many accoutrements, so you will need multiple plates, bowls, and serving pieces. Use them to tell a visual story. I serve my tortillas in a natural woven basket—to reflect the handcrafted aesthetic of Mexico—and incorporate varying shades of blue. The striped napkin adds a classic coastal vibe, while the teal glassware and ceramics evoke the sea.

GRILLED FLUKE WITH ESCABECHE THREE WAYS

Fluke is a delicate white fish that crumbles to bits if it's cooked directly on a grill. I learned to avoid that fate from an unlikely source. I'm mildly embarrassed to share it, but it's just too good not to. Years ago, while visiting a friend, I found his copy of *Grilling for Dummies*, which had an illustration of fish grilled on a bed of lemons. The technique simultaneously prevents sticking and infuses the flesh with citrusy flavor—and it's been my go-to method for any delicate fish ever since.

Escabeche is a punchy Spanish sauce typically applied to seafood after it's taken off the heat. I've included three variations here to illustrate how easy it is to create multiple personas for a simple piece of fish.

SERVES 4 TO 6

—

4 to 6 large lemons (1 for each fish fillet)

2 pounds (910 g) fluke (4 to 6 fillets)

Extra-virgin olive oil

Salt and freshly cracked pepper

PEACH-CORN ESCABECHE

⅓ cup (75 ml) extra-virgin olive oil

¼ cup (60 ml) champagne vinegar

1 lemon, zested and juiced

½ teaspoon kosher salt

1 ripe but firm white peach, halved, pitted, and cut into ¼-inch (6-mm) slices

2 ears white corn, kernels removed

½ cup (30 g) finely chopped green onions, white and light green parts only (5 to 6 onions)

½ teaspoon minced serrano chile

8 large fresh basil leaves, torn into pieces

CONTINUED ON PAGE 109

Preheat the grill over medium-high heat to about 400°F (205°C). Cut each lemon into five slices, discarding the ends. Drizzle the fish with olive oil and season with salt and pepper.

Lay the lemon slices on the grill in clusters of five. Place one fillet on each bed of lemon slices, tucking the thin end of the fillet under to help the fish cook evenly. Be sure the fish is not touching the grill. Close the lid and grill the fish until it's just cooked through, 6 to 8 minutes. Using a wide spatula, carefully scoop the fish and lemons off the grill. Serve with any of the following escabeche marinades.

To make the peach-corn escabeche: In a bowl, whisk together the oil, vinegar, lemon juice and zest, and salt. Add the peaches, corn, green onions, chile, and basil. Gently toss together and set aside until ready to use.

swoon tip

Presentation wise, do not overdo it with the sauces; less is more! Spoon whichever escabeche you choose sparingly across the width of the fillets; you want to be mindful of the interplay of color, texture, and pattern, and keep some negative space on the plate. You can serve any extra sauce in a small bowl, allowing your guests to add as much as they'd like.

OREGANO AND RED ONION
ESCABECHE

3 tablespoons red wine vinegar

1 lemon, juiced

½ teaspoon kosher salt

1 cup (125 g) thinly sliced red onion

½ cup (120 ml) extra-virgin olive oil

5 sprigs fresh oregano, leaves roughly
  chopped (about 2 tablespoons)

1 tablespoon capers, roughly chopped

2½ teaspoons finely chopped Fresno
  chile

TARRAGON-LIME ESCABECHE

1 clove garlic

½ teaspoon kosher salt

½ cup (120 ml) extra-virgin olive oil

2 limes, zested and juiced

1 cup (50 g) packed fresh tarragon
  leaves, finely chopped

½ cup (25 g) packed fresh parsley
  leaves, finely chopped

½ teaspoon minced jalapeño (optional)

Sliced Fresno chile (optional)

Flaky sea salt and freshly cracked
  pepper

To make the oregano and red onion escabeche: In a bowl, whisk together the vinegar, lemon juice, and salt. Add the red onions and let it sit for 10 minutes. Add the oil, oregano, capers, and chile and stir to combine. Set aside until ready to use.

To make the tarragon-lime escabeche: With a mortar and pestle, mash the garlic and salt together into a paste.

In a bowl, whisk together the oil, lime juice and zest, and mashed garlic. Add the tarragon, parsley, and chiles, if using, and stir to combine. Season with salt and pepper. Set aside until ready to use.

GRILLED SEAFOOD PAELLA

When your hubby is a tech-house DJ, it's safe to say that you'll spend part of your summer in Ibiza. And aside from the nightlife, the Spanish island has another claim to fame: paella. I never get tired of it. Paella really does have it all: veggies, grains, chorizo, and seafood so fresh that you can taste the ocean in every bite. The trick to making a robust paella is the sofrito, the dish's saucy, oniony base. If you take the time to develop its flavors, you will be richly rewarded for your efforts.

SERVES 8 TO 10

—

1½ pounds (680 g) littleneck clams

1 pound (455 g) mussels

1 pound (455 g) head-on jumbo shrimp (about 14)

½ cup (120 ml) olive oil, plus more for drizzling

3 teaspoons kosher salt, divided

2 teaspoons smoked paprika, divided

6 cups (1.4 L) chicken stock, plus extra as needed

Large pinch saffron threads (about ½ teaspoon)

10 ounces (280 g) dried Spanish chorizo, chopped

2 leeks, white and light green parts only, halved lengthwise and thinly sliced

1 onion, finely chopped

4 cloves garlic, chopped

1 Fresno chile, seeded and minced

½ red bell pepper, finely chopped

2 medium summer squash, quartered and cut into ¼-inch (6-mm) strips

2 sprigs fresh thyme

¾ cup (180 ml) dry white wine

4 plum tomatoes, grated on a box grater, skin discarded

1 tablespoon tomato paste

3 cups (570 g) short-grain Spanish rice, such as Bomba or Arborio

2 lemons, 1 halved and 1 cut into wedges

Small handful fresh parsley, finely chopped, for serving

Scrub the clams under cold water. Transfer them to a large bowl and cover with cold, very heavily salted water and soak for 2 to 4 hours in the refrigerator to express any sand.

Scrub and debeard the mussels. Transfer them to a bowl and cover loosely with a damp paper towel; place in the refrigerator. Place the shrimp in a bowl and drizzle with the olive oil. Toss with 1 teaspoon of the salt and 1 teaspoon of the paprika. Place in the refrigerator.

Pour the stock into a medium saucepan and sprinkle it with the saffron, crumbling it between your fingers. Heat over medium heat until warm and steaming.

Preheat the grill over medium-high heat to 400°F (205°C). Heat the olive oil in a 16-inch (40.5-cm) paella pan. Add the chorizo and cook, stirring occasionally, until most of the fat has rendered, about 5 minutes.

Add the leeks and onion to the pan and sauté, stirring occasionally, until soft and translucent, about 3 minutes. Add the garlic and chile and sauté for 1 minute. Add the bell pepper, squash, thyme, the remaining 2 teaspoons salt, and the remaining 1 teaspoon paprika. Cook, stirring occasionally, until the vegetables have softened, about 4 minutes. Pour in the wine and scrape up any browned bits that may have stuck to the bottom of the pan. Cook until most of the wine has evaporated, about 1 minute. Stir in the tomatoes and tomato paste and cook, stirring occasionally, for 5 minutes.

Add the rice to the pan and toast, stirring occasionally, 2 to 3 minutes. Pour in the warm stock and stir to combine. Do not stir the paella from this point on. Close the grill and cook for 15 minutes.

Bury the clams and mussels in the rice and press the shrimp on top. If the rice seems dry, add another ½ cup (120 ml) of chicken stock. Loosely tent the pan with foil. Close the grill lid and cook until all of the clams and mussels have opened and the shrimp is opaque, 12 to 15 minutes. (Discard any clams or mussels that haven't opened.) Remove the paella from the heat and cover tightly with foil. Let it sit for 10 minutes.

Just before serving, squeeze the lemon halves over the paella and sprinkle with parsley. Serve with lemon wedges on the side.

swoon tip — What could be more dramatic than carrying a giant, sizzling pan straight from the fire to the table? That's the allure of paella, so don't even think about plating it! This perfectly organic composition of seafood is a bona fide natural beauty. Adding a few bright lemon wedges and a handful of chopped parsley is as far as I'd go in terms of gussying it up.

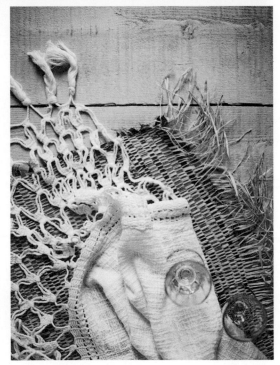

CEDAR-GRILLED HALIBUT
WITH PRESERVED-LEMON-AND-FENNEL RELISH

I love grilling on a cedar plank—the wood provides a stable surface on which to gently steam any hearty fish, keeping it tender and moist while infusing it with fantastic, woodsy flavor. Here, I pair halibut with a preserved-lemon-and-fennel relish that I came up with while riffing and playing in a friend's kitchen—my favorite way to cook. I also serve this fish with a simple salsa verde, like the one on page 266. My son, for one, is obsessed with the combination. Either way, be sure to soak your cedar plank in water for at least an hour before placing it on the grill so that it doesn't dry out and burn during cooking.

SERVES 4

—

FOR THE RELISH

¼ cup (60 ml) fresh lemon juice
(about 2 large lemons)

3 tablespoons extra-virgin olive oil

2 tablespoons champagne vinegar

2 teaspoons honey

1 tablespoon finely chopped fresh dill,
plus more for garnish

3 teaspoons finely chopped jalapeño

1 preserved lemon (store-bought, or
see recipe on page 269), rind only,
finely chopped

⅔ cup (55 g) finely chopped fennel

Salt and freshly cracked pepper

FOR THE HALIBUT AND TOMATOES

1 (7 x 15-inch/17 x 38-cm) cedar
plank

4 (6- to 8-ounce/170- to 225-g)
halibut fillets, skin removed

Extra-virgin olive oil

Salt and freshly cracked pepper

2 pints (20 to 24 ounces/560 to 680 g)
Sun Gold cherry tomatoes

2 teaspoons champagne vinegar

½ lemon

Make the relish: In a medium bowl, whisk together the lemon juice, oil, vinegar, and honey. Stir in the dill, jalapeño, and preserved lemon. Add the fennel and toss until it's evenly coated. Season with salt and pepper and set aside. The chutney can be made an hour or two in advance, but is best when it's fresh and bright.

Make the halibut and tomatoes: Preheat the grill over medium-high heat to about 400°F (205°C). Drizzle the fish with oil and season with salt and pepper. Lay the cedar plank on the grill and place the fish on the plank. Close the lid of the grill and cook for 8 minutes. Meanwhile, place the tomatoes in a cast-iron skillet. Drizzle with oil and season with salt and pepper. Place the skillet on the grill next to the cedar plank and close the lid. Continue to cook until the fish is just opaque throughout and the tomatoes have begun to burst, 6 to 7 minutes. Drizzle the tomatoes with the vinegar and cook 1 minute more.

Transfer the fish to a serving platter and scatter it with the tomatoes. Spoon some of the relish around the fish, garnish with chopped dill, and finish with a squeeze of lemon. Serve with extra relish on the side.

The beauty of cooking on a cedar plank is that the fillet stays intact and immaculate, without char marks or broken bits from flipping. To play up the fish's pristine presentation, serve it on a simple white plate, surrounded—but not covered by—the colorful relish.

GRILLED CLAMS WITH JALAPEÑO-HERB BUTTER

If there is any one dish that embodies the low-key essence of summer by the sea, it might just be grilled clams. We are fortunate to live super close to the bay beach, so raking up these bad boys for a last-minute feast is practically effortless. After throwing them in a woven bag, into my bike basket they go, only to be tossed onto a smoking grill—it's a meal in minutes. Once the clams are cooked, I dot them with scrumptious herb-flecked jalapeño butter, which melts into their briny juices to form a delicious sauce. You'll want to sop up every last drop with some toasted baguette, which might just be the most delicious part.

SERVES 4 TO 6

—

1 stick (4 ounces/115 g) unsalted butter, at room temperature

3 green onions, finely chopped

1 clove garlic, minced

1 jalapeño, seeds removed, minced

¼ cup (10 g) fresh basil, finely chopped

¼ cup (13 g) fresh parsley, finely chopped

1 lime, zested and juiced

½ teaspoon kosher salt

24 littleneck clams, scrubbed and rinsed

1 baguette, sliced and toasted, for serving

In a small bowl, mix together the butter, onions, garlic, jalapeño, basil, parsley, lime zest, and salt. If you're not using the jalapeño butter immediately, refrigerate it until ready to use. Just before serving, gently melt the butter in a saucepan over low heat.

Preheat a grill over medium-high heat to about 400°F (205°C). Place the clams directly on the grill. Cook just until the clams pop open, 5 to 6 minutes. Remove them to a platter or newspaper, discarding any clams that do not open. Spoon a little jalapeño butter over each clam and drizzle them with the lime juice. Serve the clams with toasted slices of baguette and the remaining butter on the side.

Sometimes, when plating, you need to think beyond the plate. Play up the casual vibe of this dish by spilling the clams out onto newspaper. There's something inherently festive about eating straight off the table, classic clambake style. Bonus: The paper soaks up the greasy drips.

GREEN PANZANELLA
WITH GRILLED CHICKEN PAILLARDS

Let's face it: Grilled chicken is one of those go-to weeknight summer meals that requires little thought—which is precisely its appeal. And a paillard is one of the least complex and most user-friendly food preparations ever. It's just a piece of meat pounded thin and cooked on the grill; *paillard* may as well be French for "effortless." Chicken aside, the true star of this recipe is the panzanella salad. It's a vibrant showcase for late-summer green tomatoes, crunchy cukes, and the even crunchier croutons that absorb the dish's perfectly pungent juices. And as a bonus, panzanella is also a great way to use up day-old bread!

SERVES 4

—

FOR THE CHICKEN

3 cloves garlic, chopped

2 sprigs fresh oregano, chopped

2 lemons, zested and juiced

2 tablespoons extra-virgin olive oil

1 teaspoon kosher salt

20 grinds freshly cracked pepper

½ teaspoon sugar

4 (5-ounce/140-g) chicken breasts, pounded thin, about ¼ inch (6 mm) thick

FOR THE SALAD

1½ lemons, juiced

3 tablespoons red wine vinegar

½ cup (120 ml) extra-virgin olive oil, plus more for drizzling

Salt and freshly cracked pepper

4 cups (360 g) 1-inch (2.5-cm) cubes ciabatta or country bread

3 large green heirloom tomatoes (about 1½ pounds/680 g total), cut into wedges

2 Kirby cucumbers, thinly sliced into rounds

1 small clove garlic, minced

½ red onion, thinly sliced

1 small bunch fresh parsley, torn

1 small bunch fresh basil, torn

1 sprig fresh oregano, chopped

Make the chicken: In a baking dish, stir together the garlic, oregano, lemon juice and zest, oil, salt, pepper, and sugar (to help with the browning). Coat the chicken with the marinade; cover it with plastic wrap and let it marinate at room temperature for 15 to 20 minutes.

Heat a grill over medium-high heat. Remove the chicken from the marinade and season it with salt and pepper. Grill the chicken until it's lightly charred and cooked through, about 3 minutes per side.

Make the dressing: In a small bowl, whisk together the lemon juice and vinegar. Slowly whisk in the olive oil. Season with salt and pepper.

Preheat the oven to 400°F (205°C). Spread the ciabatta on a baking sheet and drizzle it with olive oil. Toss to coat. Bake until crisp and lightly golden, about 10 minutes total, tossing the bread about halfway through.

In a medium bowl, toss the tomatoes, cucumbers, garlic, red onion, and toasted ciabatta with enough dressing to coat. Gently fold in the herbs and season to taste. Serve the green panzanella on top of the grilled chicken.

swoon tip

The trick to getting distinct, picture-perfect grill marks: Make sure your grill is screaming hot and your chicken breasts are uniformly thin, allowing for even contact with the heat. Ask your butcher to preslice the cutlets or pound them thin yourself between two pieces of plastic wrap using a meat mallet or the side of a can. To avoid breaking up the meat, be sure to concentrate on the middle as well as the outer edges.

LAMB KEFTE WITH TZATZIKI

I grew up steeped in the tradition of the Italian-American meatball. While I still savor its flavor when I go home to my mama's for Sunday sauce, I have never really been a traditionalist in my own kitchen. These lamb kefte express the dynamic flavors I swoon over; Middle Eastern in origin, they contain a mélange of pine nuts, fresh herbs, and bold, unexpected spices that makes them irresistible! Whether it's Italian or Middle Eastern, a perfect meatball's essential ingredient is moisture. And so I've bound these guys together with milk-soaked bulgur; though it's an unorthodox grain to find in a meatball, it adds a light, juicy element to the ground meat.

Although summer cooking demands perfectly charred grill marks on meat, you can also cook the kefte in a broiler on the highest setting.

MAKES ABOUT 25 MEATBALLS
SERVES 6
—

½ cup (120 ml) whole milk, heated
  until steaming
¼ cup (35 g) coarse bulgur
1½ pounds (680 g) ground lamb
1 large egg
1 onion, very finely chopped
3 cloves garlic, minced
⅓ cup (17 g) finely chopped fresh
  parsley
⅓ cup plus 2 tablespoons (60 g)
  toasted pine nuts
2 teaspoons ground cumin
1 teaspoon paprika
½ teaspoon ground allspice
¼ teaspoon cayenne pepper
1½ teaspoons kosher salt
Freshly cracked pepper

FOR SERVING
Grilled flatbread (page 270), warmed
Tzatziki Sauce (page 267)
Roughly chopped or torn fresh herbs
  such as parsley, mint, and dill

In a small bowl, pour the hot milk over the bulgur and cover with plastic wrap. Let it stand for 15 to 20 minutes to soften.

Combine the remaining ingredients in a large bowl, reserving 2 tablespoons of the pine nuts for garnish. Add the soaked bulgur along with its excess milk, and mix to combine. Shape the mixture into oval meatballs about the size of a small egg.

Preheat a grill over medium-high heat to about 400°F (205°C). Grill the meatballs in batches until cooked through and lightly charred on all sides, about 12 minutes total.

Serve the meatballs on a piece of warmed flatbread spread with tzatziki, with plenty of torn fresh herbs and a scattering of the reserved pine nuts. Serve extra tzatziki on the side.

This meal is meant to be a super-casual, DIY affair—think of it as a Middle Eastern version of a taco bar. In keeping with that laid-back vibe, none of the components should look overly perfect or manicured. Shape the flatbread into organic, irregular forms and allow the fresh mint and dill to retain a bit of their natural wildness.

GRILLED RIB-EYE
WITH BURST TOMATOES AND CHIMICHURRI

Grilling season wouldn't be complete without throwing a juicy steak on the fire. Neither I nor my carnivore of a son will ever turn down a succulent rib-eye, especially when it's served with fresh chimichurri! A mélange of peppery arugula, bright parsley, garlic, shallots, and hot red pepper, the Argentinean sauce provides just the right acidic contrast to the rich meat—think of it as the yin to the steak's yang. Some blistered summer tomatoes, still clinging to their vine, bring the plate that much closer to perfection.

SERVES 4

—

2 boneless rib-eye steaks, about 1½ inches (4 cm) thick, left at room temperature for 1 hour before grilling

Salt and freshly cracked pepper

2 stems on-the-vine cherry tomatoes (there are about 10 tomatoes per vine)

Extra-virgin olive oil, for drizzling, plus extra for the grill

Chimichurri (page 267), for serving

Oil the grill grate and preheat the grill over high heat to about 450°F (230°C). Pat the steaks dry and season them with salt and pepper. Grill 6 to 7 minutes per side for medium-rare.

While the steaks are grilling, place the tomatoes in a cast-iron skillet, drizzle them with olive oil, and season with salt and pepper. When you flip your steaks, place the skillet on the grill. Grill until the tomatoes have just begun to burst, 7 to 8 minutes.

Let the steak rest for 5 minutes before serving with the burst tomatoes and chimichurri sauce on the side.

swoon tip

Food has a personality and that story should be reflected in how you serve it. Argentinean steak with chimichurri is the ultimate cowboy meal, so it makes sense to present it on a time-worn wooden board. Here, cherry tomatoes on the vine—which have a beautifully sculptural quality—add a little elegance to the rough-and-tumble vibe.

SMOKY AND SPICY PORK RIBS

Sticky fingers, tender meat sucked off the bone, and a messy face to boot—bring it on, summer! I love the primal act of sinking my teeth into a meaty pile of ribs, just off the grill. But while I've always craved a finger-lickin' rack of baby backs, I didn't make them at home very often until I developed this complex, smoky-spicy sauce. Now I'm absurdly addicted.

This recipe does require some prep time, but the sauce can be made well in advance—it keeps for weeks. (Double it if you can. It's really good.) Likewise, the ribs allow some flexibility in timing. You cook them low and slow in the oven until they're über-tender but not quite falling off the bone. At this stage, they can sit for a few hours until you're ready to finish them on the grill. One caution: The sauce can cause a bit of a flare-up, so be sure to keep an eye on the grill.

SERVES 6

—

FOR THE RIBS

½ cup (110 g) packed dark brown sugar

3 tablespoons smoked paprika

1½ teaspoons cayenne pepper

40 grinds freshly cracked pepper

2½ tablespoons kosher salt

6 pounds (2.7 kg) baby back ribs, membrane removed (ask your butcher to do this)

FOR THE SAUCE

1½ sticks (6 ounces/170 g) unsalted butter

8 cloves garlic, minced

½ cup (120 ml) cider vinegar

1½ tablespoons mirin

1½ tablespoons minced fresh ginger

Roast the ribs: Preheat the oven to 300°F (150°C). In a bowl, mix together the sugar, paprika, cayenne, pepper, and salt. Transfer about a third of the spice mixture to a small bowl and set it aside; it will be used for the sticky sauce.

Lay a large piece of foil on a work surface. Working with one rack at a time, place the ribs on the foil and rub them on all sides with some of the remaining spice mixture. Fold up the foil around the ribs, using one or two additional pieces of foil to make a sealed, sturdy packet. Repeat with the remaining rack(s). Place the packets on a baking sheet and roast until the meat is very tender, 2½ to 3 hours.

Make the sauce: While the ribs are roasting, in a medium saucepan, melt the butter over low heat. Whisk in the garlic, vinegar, mirin, ginger, and the reserved spice mixture. Simmer over low heat, stirring occasionally, until the sauce has thickened and reduced by half, about 20 minutes.

Grill the ribs: When the ribs are done, carefully open the packets and transfer the meat to a clean baking sheet. Pour any juices that have accumulated in the packets into a measuring cup; use a spoon to skim the fat from the top. Whisk the juices into the sticky sauce and simmer until the sauce has thickened slightly, about 10 minutes.

Preheat a grill over medium heat to about 400°F (205°C). Brush the ribs on all sides with the sauce. Grill until the ribs are lightly charred, about 4 minutes per side. Brush with the remaining sauce before cutting the ribs into portions and serving.

Ribs are never a neat and tidy affair, which is part of why we love them. Rather than attempting to achieve perfectly even pieces, honor their sticky, gooey spirit by jumbling together single, double, and triple-rib portions on a simple platter—and don't dream of wiping up the saucy drips.

LIME-RASPBERRY TART

Lime and raspberry are quite the dynamic duo, mouth-puckeringly tart, sweet, and refreshing all at once. In this tart, they team up with a truly amazing confectioners' sugar–based pastry that I discovered through Smitten Kitchen's Deb Perelman, who adapted it from baking guru Dorie Greenspan. And I've adapted it yet again by adding poppy seeds to the dough—I love the subtle black accents and unexpected crunch they add.

SERVES 8

—

FOR THE LIME CURD

5 large egg yolks

⅔ cup (135 g) granulated sugar

1½ tablespoons lime zest

½ cup (120 ml) fresh lime juice (from about 5 juicy limes)

⅛ teaspoon kosher salt

1 stick (4 ounces/115 g) unsalted butter, cut into 8 pieces

FOR THE DOUGH

1½ cups (190 g) all-purpose flour, plus more for rolling out the dough

½ cup (65 g) confectioners' sugar

¼ teaspoon kosher salt

1½ tablespoons poppy seeds, plus more for garnish, if desired

1 stick (4 ounces/115 g) unsalted butter, cut into cubes and frozen, plus 1 tablespoon kept soft for buttering the tart pan

1 large egg, lightly beaten

6 ounces (170 g) fresh raspberries, for topping

6 ounces (170 g) white currants or more raspberries, for topping

Make the lime curd: Place a fine-mesh sieve over a medium bowl and position it near the stovetop. Bring a pot of shallow water to a gentle simmer.

In a metal bowl, whisk together the egg yolks, granulated sugar, and lime zest until thick and pale, about 2 minutes. Whisk in the lime juice and salt. Set the bowl over the simmering water. The bottom of the bowl should hover an inch or two above the water's surface. Whisking constantly, cook until the curd coats the back of a spoon, 5 to 7 minutes (or until an instant-read thermometer registers 165 to 170°F/75 to 77°C). Remove the curd from the heat and press it through the sieve into a clean bowl. Add the butter to the curd; let it stand 1 minute. Stir to combine. If the butter doesn't totally melt, let the curd rest another 1 to 2 minutes and stir again.

Place a piece of plastic wrap directly onto the surface of the curd. Let it cool to room temperature, then refrigerate until chilled, at least 4 hours. The curd may be made up to 2 days in advance.

Make the dough: Place the flour, confectioners' sugar, salt, and poppy seeds in the bowl of a food processor and pulse to combine. Add the cold butter and pulse until it is in pea-sized pieces. Add the egg and pulse just until the dough comes together. If the dough has dry patches, add 1 tablespoon ice water and pulse again. Transfer the dough to a clean work surface and press it into a round. Wrap it in plastic and refrigerate for at least 2 hours or overnight.

Make the tart: On a lightly floured surface, roll the dough into a ¼-inch-thick (6-mm-thick) round. Use the tablespoon of soft butter to grease a 9-inch (23-cm) fluted tart pan with a removable bottom. Press the dough into the bottom and sides of the pan. Trim the dough, leaving a ½-inch (12-mm) overhang. Fold the overhang underneath the dough and pinch together to reinforce the sides. Using a fork, pierce the bottom of the crust all over. Freeze for 1 hour.

Preheat the oven to 375°F (190°C). Bake the crust until golden and crisp, 25 to 30 minutes. Let it cool completely.

Pour the lime curd into the tart shell. Refrigerate, uncovered, for at least 2 hours. When ready to serve, top with the raspberries and currants, if using.

To accentuate the contrast between the pale pink currants and the shocking pink raspberries, I chose a platter and linens that fall in between the two on the color spectrum. If you don't happen to have a pink plate, a few glasses of rosy champagne will provide the same tone-on-tone beauty.

GRILLED PLUMS WITH PISTACHIO BRITTLE

It's hard to find something more casual—or more ideal for an impromptu barbeque—than grilled stone fruit. I've discovered that tossing some plums or peaches on a grill blows people's minds. Maybe it's because it's unexpected, or maybe it's because it's so easy to elevate a simple piece of fruit to a superstar dessert with the touch of a little heat!

While the pistachio brittle requires a little more investment, it offers plenty in return: It keeps for weeks, so you can easily make it in advance. Though I pair it with crème fraîche here, it's also a natural partner for ice cream.

SERVES 8

—

FOR THE BRITTLE

Neutral oil cooking spray such as vegetable or canola

1 cup (200 g) sugar

¼ cup (60 ml) honey

¼ cup (60 ml) corn syrup

1 cup (130 g) roasted, unsalted pistachios, roughly chopped

1 tablespoon unsalted butter

1 teaspoon kosher salt

¾ teaspoon baking soda

Flaky sea salt, for sprinkling

FOR THE WHIPPED CRÈME FRAÎCHE

1 cup (240 ml) heavy cream

1 tablespoon sugar

½ teaspoon vanilla extract

⅓ cup (75 ml) crème fraîche

Generous pinch kosher salt

FOR THE PLUMS

¼ cup (50 g) sugar

1 lemon, zested

A couple sprigs fresh thyme, leaves roughly chopped

6 ripe but firm red plums, halved and pitted

Canola oil, for brushing the plums

Make the brittle: Line a baking sheet with parchment paper and spray the parchment with non-stick spray. Place the sugar, honey, corn syrup, and 3 tablespoons water in a medium saucepan. Measure the remaining ingredients into a bowl and place it next to the stovetop along with an oiled, heatproof spatula.

Place the saucepan over medium heat, swirling it occasionally to help dissolve the sugar.

Fit a candy thermometer on the side of the saucepan and cook the sugar syrup over medium heat until the caramel reaches 300°F (150°C), about 5 minutes. Remove the pan from the heat. Quickly stir in the pistachios, butter, salt, and baking soda until just combined.

Pour the caramel mixture onto the parchment paper and spread it with the oiled spatula so the brittle is about ¼ inch (6 mm) thick. Sprinkle the surface with flaky sea salt. Set aside and let it cool completely. Break the brittle into small, bite-size pieces and store them at room temperature in an airtight container, with the layers separated by parchment paper to prevent sticking, until ready to serve. Stored this way, the brittle will keep for a few weeks.

Make the whipped crème fraîche: In the bowl of a mixer fitted with the whisk attachment, whip the cream, sugar, and vanilla extract until medium-stiff peaks form. Add the crème fraîche and salt and whip to combine. Refrigerate until ready to serve. The whipped crème fraîche will keep for a few hours; if it loses its body, you can whip it again before serving.

Make the plums: Heat the grill over medium heat to about 375°F (190°C). In a small bowl, mix together the sugar, lemon zest, and thyme. You can rub the thyme between your fingers to help release its oils.

Lightly brush the cut sides of the plums with oil and sprinkle them with the sugar mixture. Place the plums cut-side down on the grill and cook until lightly charred and caramelized, 4 to 5 minutes. Flip and grill until tender, another 3 to 4 minutes.

Place the grilled plums on a serving platter. Top with the whipped crème fraîche and sprinkle with the brittle. Serve any extra whipped cream and brittle on the side.

Don't be afraid to break out the hammer for the brittle. I have seen many a chef use this mildly barbaric technique! Not only is it effective, it also creates jagged, asymmetrical pieces that look especially beautiful when they're juxtaposed with the soft contours of the plums and crème fraîche.

PEACH AND BLACKBERRY CROSTATAS

These free-form stunners ooze rustic sophistication, but they're practically foolproof: Just toss any ripe, seasonal fruit with some sugar, acid, and herbs; haphazardly fold and pinch the pastry; and you're golden! Here, I used peaches and blackberries—a deliciously sweet-sour combo that's hard to beat. Adding another layer of flavor is the crust, which gets its distinct tang and tender flakiness from apple cider vinegar. The dough recipe can easily be doubled and also does well in the freezer for about a month.

Although I often make four mini crostatas from this recipe, you can just as easily do one large version instead. And a little dollop of ice cream or crème fraîche on the side never hurt anyone . . .

MAKES 4 MINI CROSTATAS
—

FOR THE DOUGH

1½ cups (190 g) all-purpose flour
1 tablespoon granulated sugar
½ teaspoon kosher salt
1 stick (4 ounces/115 g) unsalted butter, frozen and cut into small pieces
1 tablespoon apple cider vinegar
¼ cup (60 ml) ice water
1 large egg, beaten, for egg wash
Turbinado sugar, for sprinkling

FOR THE FILLING

3 tablespoons granulated sugar
½ teaspoon fresh thyme leaves
3 ripe but firm peaches, halved, pitted, and cut into ½-inch (12-mm) wedges
6 ounces (170 g) fresh blackberries
⅛ teaspoon kosher salt
1 teaspoon lemon zest
1 tablespoon fresh lemon juice
½ teaspoon vanilla extract
2 teaspoons all-purpose flour

Make the dough: Place the flour, sugar, and salt in the bowl of a food processor and pulse to combine. Add the butter and pulse until the butter is in pea-size pieces. In a small bowl, combine the vinegar and ice water. Slowly pour the vinegar water into the food processor, pulsing to combine. Pulse just until the dough begins to hold together. Transfer it to a clean work surface and pat together. Shape the dough into a round and cut it into four equal pieces. Wrap each piece in plastic wrap and refrigerate them for at least 1 hour and up to 2 days.

Make the filling: Preheat the oven to 375°F (190°C). In a small bowl, rub the sugar and thyme together with your fingers to release the herb's oils. Place the peaches and blackberries in a medium bowl. Sprinkle the thyme sugar, salt, lemon zest and juice, vanilla extract, and flour over the fruit. Toss to coat.

Roll each piece of dough into a ¼-inch-thick (6-mm-thick) round and transfer it to a parchment-lined baking sheet. Divide the fruit evenly between the circles, mounding it into the center of the dough and leaving a 1½-inch (4-cm) border all around. Fold the edges up around the filling. Brush the edges of the dough with the egg wash and sprinkle them with the turbinado sugar. Bake until the crust is golden brown and the fruit is bubbling, 30 to 35 minutes.

swoon tip Don't worry too much about precision or uniformity when shaping these treats. Instead, play up their rustic beauty by serving them directly on parchment: The raw sugar becomes beautifully burnished on the paper while the oozing juices add a sensuous messiness.

THE

SUMMER

TABLE

The warm, neutral palette of the beach sets the tone for my
summer feast, with sand-colored plates, seagrass seating, and
foraged beach finds making their way onto the table. The
only blooms to speak of are wispy wildflowers, clipped from
a nearby field, and blossoming bundles of local herbs, which
ward off buzzing pests while making a visual statement. The
real star of this show is the evening sun, refracted enchantingly
through patterned glassware onto a sea-blue linen runner.
At the peak of summer, there's no competing with Mother
Nature's beauty—and why would you want to?

No.1
SHARE THE LOVE

I make berry crostata for just about every summer gathering—and I can't tell you how many times I've been asked for my recipe. A handwritten recipe card—along with a pint of local fruit—serves as a sweet takeaway for guests.

No.2
CLIP, SNIP, AND FORAGE

I appreciate the artistry that goes into fancy floral arrangements, but more often than not, I forgo the florist shop and head into my backyard with a pair of clippers instead. Some of my favorite trimmings are sprigs from my blueberry bush—they're almost more beautiful when unripe—which I display in earthy ceramic vessels.

No.3
BOTTLE SERVICE

Serving infused water in a collection of simple glass vessels—from olive oil carafes to Ikea finds—is both beautiful and practical. Elevate the ordinary by suspending a few sculptural herbs or clean-tasting veggies in bottles of varied shapes and heights. The effect is both pleasing to the eye and refreshing on the palate.

No.4
THINK OUTSIDE THE VASE

Get creative when selecting a vessel for your flowers. In lieu of a standard glass vase, I love to pile wildflowers and fragrant herbs into wooden salad bowls. Add a little water to keep the blooms fresh and don't worry too much about arranging them—the vibe should be wild and organic.

No.5
CATCH SOME RAYS

Don't overlook the power of the sun. Textured glassware filled with water sparkles in summer's early evening light, reflecting dappled, dancing shadows on an outdoor table. Meanwhile, everyone's favorite summer wine, rosé, casts the prettiest pink glow.

No.6
BUZZ OFF

Aromatic lavender and sage naturally repel summer's most unwelcome dinner guests: mosquitos and flies. When bundled tightly and tied with twine, their silvery green leaves and purple blossoms also add a decorative touch to the table.

No.7
BACK TO NATURE

Look to your surroundings to inform your décor. Before a beach feast, take a stroll along the shoreline, collecting a variety of natural treasures. Beautifully patinaed shells, sea-tumbled driftwood, and smooth beach glass lend gorgeous texture to a summer tablescape.

No.8
IN THE MIX

When it comes to flatware, a jumble of shapes and styles always looks more interesting than a matched set. Consider buying a mix of vintage pieces from a thrift shop or flea market, or take my approach and collect them over time, picking up pretty pieces as you find them.

No.9
GET CRAFTY

Handmade touches give a table personality and soul. Here, my son and I got crafty, pouring melted wax into clamshells we gathered from the beach. It's a DIY in keeping with my entertaining mantra: simple ideas, thoughtfully executed.

FALL

AUTUMN, WITHOUT A DOUBT, is my favorite time of year. I always look forward to September's busyness and structure, its exciting sense of newness and discovery.

For my family, fall means not only back to school, but back to the city and the endless sources of inspiration that my hometown has to offer. My favorite, of course, are the restaurants. When I was learning to cook, the Brooklyn restaurant scene was one of my greatest teachers. It was the beginning of the borough's culinary renaissance and Victor and I would eat out most nights at places like Franny's, Frankie's, and Marlow & Sons. I'd spend the next day gathering groceries and attempting—through trial and error and lots of Googling—to re-create the dishes I'd fallen in love with the night before. A decade later, not much has changed. My first weeks back to urban life are punctuated with reservations at both my old favorites and the new kids on the block, followed by some serious time in front of the stove.

Every year, as the air teeters from warm to crisp, all the familiar autumn cravings come flooding back. After summer's endless raw salads, we long for soul-warming soups. We return to our ovens and roast everything from pork shoulder and chicken breasts to squash and cauliflower. In autumn I begin to feel like a sorceress in the kitchen, simmering and stirring as I layer textures and try out new flavor profiles.

And my experiments aren't limited to my own kitchen. One of my favorite places to cook in the fall is at Westwind Orchard, my dear friends Laura and Fabio's organic farm in Upstate New York. In September and October their thirty-two-acre property is engulfed in a blaze of foliage and bursting at the seams with fall bounty. I love to meander around picking fruit and veggies and sampling the farm's own honey and maple syrup. Savoring those last frost-free days, we lay out picnic blankets under the canopy of colorful leaves and feast on creamy ricotta toasts and cake made from apples fresh off the orchard trees.

Spending time at Westwind, I'm always reminded of food's power to bring people together. Just a few years ago, Laura and Fabio were complete strangers. Today, bonded by our shared passion for cooking and gathering around the table, they are part of my ever-expanding food family. As I stand by their kitchen door, I can hear our kids laughing while they make apple cider, climb trees, and zip around like daredevils on the quads. Between the company and the scenery—the light and leaves turning golden, the sky so brilliant blue—I'm filled with the deepest sense of warmth and belonging. Fall takes my breath away at every turn.

IN SEASON

APPLES   CRANBERRIES   PEARS

BRUSSELS   CURRANTS   POMEGRANATES
SPROUTS

                  GRAPES   PUMPKINS
CARROTS
                  JERUSALEM   WILD MUSHROOMS
CAULIFLOWER   ARTICHOKES
                                      WINTER SQUASH
CELERY   KALE
                                      BROCCOLI

ROASTED PUMPKIN AND BRUSSELS SPROUTS WITH POACHED EGGS

Potato and vegetable hash topped with a poached egg is a tried-and-true weekend staple in my house, and one that evolves with the seasons. The possibilities are endless—kale and carrots, fava beans and beets . . . but in fall, creamy, caramelized pumpkin and crispy little Brussels sprouts are a favorite variation. If you can't find pumpkin, feel free to swap in some sweet potatoes or butternut squash. Either way, do take the extra time to pull apart the sprout leaves before roasting them; you end up with a crackling texture that's well worth the trouble. If you're planning to serve this dish for company, you can poach the eggs in advance. Store them in cool water (to stop the cooking) until ready to use, and then warm them in hot water before serving.

SERVES 2

—

12 ounces (340 g) pumpkin, peeled and cut into 1-inch (2.5-cm) cubes (about 2 cups/480 ml)

8 ounces (225 g) Yukon Gold potatoes, cut into 1-inch (2.5-cm) cubes

Extra-virgin olive oil, for drizzling

Salt and freshly cracked pepper

1 pound (455 g) Brussels sprouts

1 tablespoon distilled white vinegar

2 large eggs, at room temperature

½ teaspoon finely minced habanero chile (optional)

1 small lemon, zested

1 small handful fresh parsley, minced

Flaky sea salt, for serving

Preheat the oven to 425°F (220°C). Spread the pumpkin and potatoes on a baking sheet. Drizzle them with oil, and season with salt and pepper. Roast for 15 minutes.

Peel the outer leaves of the sprouts until you get to the small, white inner leaves, trimming the sprout's bottom to help release more leaves. Place the leaves on a baking sheet, reserving the centers of the sprouts for another use. Toss the leaves with olive oil and season with salt and pepper.

Remove the pumpkin and potatoes from the oven. Toss and return them to the oven along with the sprout leaves. Roast until the vegetables are golden and tender and the leaves are crispy, 6 to 8 minutes.

While the vegetables are finishing in the oven, fill a medium saucepan halfway with water. Add the vinegar and bring it to a gentle simmer. You should see small bubbles around the bottom and edges of the pan, but do not let the water boil.

Crack an egg into a ramekin. Using a spoon, stir the water in circles to make a gentle whirl-pool. Gently pour the egg into the water. Simmer for 2 minutes, undisturbed, then remove it with a slotted spoon to a paper towel–lined plate. Repeat with the remaining egg.

Toss the roasted vegetables together with the habanero, if using. Divide them between two plates and top each with a poached egg. Sprinkle with the lemon zest, parsley, and flaky sea salt.

The secret to pretty poached eggs? Adding a little vinegar to the water, which causes the proteins in the whites to coagulate more quickly, preventing unsightly wisps. Swirling the water with the tail of a wooden spoon to create a little whirlpool also helps by drawing the egg into the center, encouraging a nice round shape. And if you happen to break a yolk while plating, don't sweat it. A sunny little pool of bright yellow creates color contrast on the plate.

CREAMY CAULIFLOWER SOUP WITH DUKKAH AND WATERCRESS PESTO

When I was a kid, my mom's pureed broccoli soup was my number one cool-weather craving. My son has clearly inherited some of my taste buds—he's obsessed with this similarly creamy cauliflower version. This soup combines sweet roasted florets with buttery Yukon Gold potatoes and an aromatic trifecta of leeks, garlic, and thyme. The key, when pureeing, is to add liquid just a little at a time. If the soup becomes too watery, there's no turning back. And to avoid a cauliflower volcano, remember to remove the center insert of your blender and cover the hole with a kitchen towel so steam can escape.

When it comes to toppings, you've got some options. The nut, seed, and spice mixture known as dukkah adds wonderful crunch, but I also love the brightness of lemony watercress-pistachio pesto, which cuts through the heavier flavors. Use both, as I have done here, or choose just one.

SERVES 4

—

1 large head cauliflower (about 2 pounds/910 g), cored and cut into bite-size florets

¼ cup (60 ml) extra-virgin olive oil, plus extra for drizzling

Kosher salt

2 leeks, white and light green parts only, cut in half lengthwise and rinsed clean

3 sprigs fresh thyme

2 cloves garlic, minced

8 ounces (225 g) Yukon Gold potatoes (about 3), peeled and quartered

3 cups (720 ml) chicken stock

⅔ cup (185 ml) heavy cream

2 lemons, zested and juiced

Freshly cracked pepper

Watercress-Pistachio Pesto (page 267), for serving

Dukkah (page 268), for serving

Preheat the oven to 425°F (220°C).

Spread the cauliflower florets on a baking sheet. Drizzle them generously with oil, season with salt, and toss to coat. Roast for 15 minutes, tossing the cauliflower halfway through. Continue to roast until golden brown, about 15 minutes more.

While the cauliflower is roasting, chop the leeks crosswise into roughly ¼-inch (6-mm) slices. In a medium saucepan, heat the oil and thyme over medium heat and sauté the leeks until they are slightly softened, about 2 minutes. Add the garlic and cook until soft and fragrant, about 2 minutes more.

Add the potatoes, stock, cream, 2 cups (480 ml) water, and the roasted cauliflower to the pot. Bring the mixture to a gentle simmer over medium-low heat and cover, cooking until the potatoes are fork tender, 15 to 20 minutes. Once the potatoes are tender, remove the thyme stems from the mixture (the leaves should have fallen off during cooking).

Transfer the mixture to a blender and cover the hole of the blender top with a towel. Blend until the mixture is very smooth. Stir in the lemon juice and season with 2 teaspoons salt and some pepper. Divide the soup among four bowls and top it with lemon zest, a swirl of the watercress pesto, and a sprinkle of dukkah.

Pureed soup can look—and taste—boringly basic without a garnish or two to liven it up. Restaurant chefs often use plastic squeeze bottles to layer on something bright or creamy, but at home there's no need to be so fussy. Just gently swirl in a minimal amount of pesto with a teaspoon, mixing only the surface of the soup in a loose circular motion.

MEYER LEMON RICOTTA TOASTS
WITH BLISTERED GRAPES

The first time I tried roasted grapes was at Franny's, one of my all-time-favorite Brooklyn restaurants, and to say I fell hard for them would be an understatement. These days, I regularly pop red and black varieties into a scorching hot oven until they're blistered and oozing with sugary juice. Roasted grapes are delicious alongside pork or rabbit, but my absolute favorite way to savor them is with fresh ricotta on crostini. The crunchy bread, jammy fruit, and creamy cheese are a decadent combination, especially when spiked with Meyer lemon zest and drizzled with saba—a syrupy Italian condiment made by cooking down grapes. My recipe isn't finicky: Rosemary would work in place of tarragon and really any type of seedless grape will do. If you can't find saba, simmer balsamic vinegar until it's reduced by half to achieve a similar taste and consistency.

SERVES 4 TO 6
—

12 ounces (340 g) seedless red or black grapes

4 sprigs fresh tarragon, divided

Extra-virgin olive oil, for drizzling

Salt and freshly cracked pepper

1 cup (240 ml) fresh ricotta

½ Meyer lemon, zested and juiced

4 slices crusty bread

3 tablespoons pine nuts, toasted

Saba or syrupy balsamic vinegar, for drizzling

Preheat the oven to 400°F (205°C). Spread the grapes across a baking sheet and top them with 2 tarragon sprigs. Drizzle with oil and toss the grapes until evenly coated. Season with salt and pepper. Roast the grapes until they have just started to burst, 15 to 20 minutes. Let cool slightly, discard the tarragon, and squeeze the lemon juice evenly over the grapes.

While the grapes are roasting, use a wire whisk to combine the ricotta and lemon zest.

Just before you're ready to serve the crostini, heat up the broiler. Place the bread on a baking sheet and drizzle it lightly with oil on both sides. Broil until golden, 1 to 2 minutes per side depending on the strength of your broiler. Let the toasts cool slightly. Pluck the leaves from the remaining tarragon sprigs. Spread the ricotta mixture over each slice of bread and top with the grapes and pine nuts. Finish with a sprinkle of tarragon and a drizzle of saba.

With gooey grapes and smeared-on ricotta, these toasts are a gorgeous mess. The only nod to order: Drizzle the sweet-sour saba on at the last second so it doesn't discolor the ricotta.

JERUSALEM ARTICHOKE, CELERY, AND PEAR SALAD

Celery is like the forgotten vegetable—no one ever thinks of it. But if I had to make just one salad all fall, it would be this one, in which celery plays a starring role. A super-crunchy showstopper with an unexpected flavor profile, this dish is dead simple to prepare. I always marvel at how the clean, pure taste of each ingredient comes through in every bite. In addition to refreshing celery, there's earthy sunchoke, sweet pear, toasty hazelnut, and briny Manchego—all of them married together with a lemony vinaigrette.

I like to serve this salad with a decadent main course, like a braise or a roast, because its zippy flavors cut through the richness. And sometimes I play around with the ingredients, subbing pecorino Toscano for the Manchego, apples for the pears, or fennel for the celery. You should feel free to do the same.

SERVES 4
—

FOR THE VINAIGRETTE

2 tablespoons apple cider vinegar

2½ tablespoons fresh lemon juice

¼ cup (60 ml) extra-virgin olive oil

Salt and freshly cracked pepper

FOR THE SALAD

12 ounces (340 g) Jerusalem
  artichokes, scrubbed

2 ripe but firm pears

5 stalks celery, thinly sliced on the
  bias, leaves reserved

2 to 3 ounces (55 to 85 g) thinly
  shaved Manchego cheese

⅓ cup (45 g) hazelnuts, toasted and
  roughly chopped

1 lemon, zested

Flaky salt, for serving

Make the vinaigrette: In a large bowl, whisk together the vinegar and lemon juice. Slowly whisk in the oil until fully combined. Season with salt and pepper.

Make the salad: Using a mandoline, shave the Jerusalem artichokes directly into the dressing. Quarter, core, and thinly slice the pears, adding them to the dressing as you go. Add the celery and half of the cheese, and toss all of the ingredients to combine. Transfer the salad to a serving platter and scatter it with the hazelnuts and the remaining cheese. Garnish with the celery leaves, lemon zest, and flaky salt.

As you slice the artichokes and pears, add them to the dressing right away to prevent them from browning. And don't throw away your celery leaves! While all too often relegated to the compost pile, their spiky shape makes them a gorgeous garnish.

TUSCAN KALE SALAD
WITH LEMON-TAHINI DRESSING

I know, I know—not another kale salad! But indulge me and try this one before you write off the world's trendiest vegetable as overrated. There are a few elements that set my kale salad apart. First, I slice the kale as thinly as possible, about $1/16$ inch (2 mm) thick. To get clean, precise cuts, I approach the leaves like basil, stacking and rolling them before chopping, chiffonade style. Second, I use apples to add a sweet-tart note to the earthy green. Finally, there's the lemon-tahini dressing, which brings everything together with its addictive, nutty acidity. After a few bites, you might just rekindle your romance with kale.

SERVES 4 TO 6
—

FOR THE DRESSING
1 clove garlic, minced
¼ teaspoon kosher salt
2 tablespoons tahini
¼ cup (60 ml) fresh lemon juice
1 teaspoon honey
3 tablespoons extra-virgin olive oil
⅛ teaspoon Aleppo pepper, plus more
  for serving

FOR THE SALAD
1 head lacinato kale, stemmed and
  thinly sliced
1 Honeycrisp apple, cored, thinly
  sliced, and cut lengthwise into
  matchsticks
⅓ cup (45 g) almonds, toasted and
  roughly chopped
2 tablespoons golden raisins
2 ounces (55 g) pecorino Toscano,
  shaved
1 lemon, zested

Make the dressing: Using the back of a heavy knife on a cutting board, mash the garlic and salt into a paste. In a small bowl, whisk together the garlic paste, tahini, lemon juice, and honey with 2 tablespoons water until a smooth paste forms. Whisk in the oil and Aleppo pepper until fully combined.

Make the salad: In a large bowl, toss together the kale, apple, almonds, and raisins. Pour the dressing over the salad and toss to coat. Top with the shaved pecorino, a sprinkle of Aleppo pepper, and the lemon zest.

Honey not only adds a sweet note to this tahini dressing, it also contains a compound that prevents oxidation, ensuring that the apples remain bright white. In fact, a quick dunk in a mixture of honey and water keeps apples from browning for up to eight hours, far longer than the more commonly used lemon juice.

SHAVED BRUSSELS SPROUTS, PINE NUTS, AND GREEN OLIVES

True story: I once got a slew of hateful comments on Instagram because I posted a photo of my son making this salad. Apparently, the fact that I let my then eleven-year-old use a mandoline was grounds for calling child protective services! But a mandoline is a necessary tool if you want to achieve the feathery, delicate sprout slivers that this salad requires. Okay, yes, the blade is sharp, but if Jivan can handle one, so can you! Be precise, watch what you're doing, and you'll be fine. And if you can find them, use larger sprouts to minimize the work. This is a super-easy fall salad that is both healthy and ridiculously delish. And there's no such thing as too much lemon here—the salt, acid, and cheese make the sprouts shine.

SERVES 4
—

FOR THE DRESSING
2 large lemons
⅓ cup (75 ml) extra-virgin olive oil
Salt and freshly cracked pepper

FOR THE SALAD
1 pound (455 g) Brussels sprouts, trimmed
¼ cup (40 g) pitted Castelvetrano olives, roughly chopped
⅔ cup (90 g) ¼-inch (6-mm) chunks pecorino Sardo cheese
¼ cup (30 g) pine nuts, toasted
Aleppo pepper, for serving (optional)
Flaky sea salt, for serving

Make the dressing: Grate the zest from 1 lemon; squeeze ⅓ cup (75 ml) juice from both lemons. In a small bowl, whisk together the lemon zest, juice, and oil. Season with salt and pepper.

Make the salad: Using a mandoline, very thinly slice the Brussels sprouts into a large bowl. Add the olives and pecorino, reserving a handful of the cheese for garnish. Drizzle the salad with the lemon dressing; toss until the Brussels sprouts are evenly coated. Taste and adjust for seasoning.

To serve, garnish with the pine nuts, remaining pecorino, and a sprinkle of Aleppo pepper, if desired. Finish with a sprinkle of flaky salt.

For beautifully golden, subtly glistening pine nuts, give them a light coating of olive oil and toast them in a pan over medium-low heat for about five minutes, stirring frequently.

DELICATA SQUASH AGRODOLCE

I am obsessed with delicata squash, plain and simple—and I do mean simple. Thanks to their tender, edible skin, prepping them is beyond easy: Just slice, scoop the seeds, and the squash rings are ready for the oven. The flesh of the delicata—which is harvested for just a few weeks in early September—is creamy and sweet, making it ideal for roasting. Once golden and caramelized, the rounds are delicious straight up, but doused with this agrodolce reduction, they're downright addictive. The syrupy sauce melds chile, honey, lime, and vinegar for a sweet, spicy, tangy flavor profile that both adults and children go crazy for.

SERVES 4

—

2 delicata squash (about 2 pounds/910 g total), seeds removed and cut into ½-inch (12-mm) rounds

3 tablespoons extra-virgin olive oil

4 tablespoons (60 ml) honey, divided

Salt and freshly cracked pepper

½ teaspoon minced red habanero chile, or 1 red Fresno chile, minced

⅓ cup (75 ml) white wine vinegar

1 large lime, grated and juiced

5 or 6 fresh sage leaves, very thinly sliced

2 tablespoons pepitas, toasted

Preheat the oven to 375°F (190°C). Place the squash in a large bowl and drizzle it with the oil and 2 tablespoons of the honey. Season with salt and pepper and toss until evenly coated.

Transfer the squash to two large rimmed baking sheets, spreading it in a single layer. Roast until golden brown, 12 to 15 minutes per side, flipping the squash halfway through baking.

Meanwhile, in a small saucepan, bring the habanero, vinegar, lime juice, and remaining 2 tablespoons honey to a boil. Season with a pinch of salt. Reduce the heat and simmer until the mixture is syrupy, 8 to 10 minutes.

Just before serving, spoon the agrodolce over the squash. Garnish with the sage, pepitas, and lime zest.

While you wouldn't necessarily want to eat the root and stem ends of a delicata squash, they're too pretty to toss. Here, they serve as a subtle accent to the dish, breaking up the visual monotony of the squash rounds with a stripy pop of color.

ROASTED CAULIFLOWER WITH LEMON ZEST, PARSLEY, CAPERS, AND JALAPEÑO

Roasted cauliflower has a nutty, sweet flavor that's hard to resist. My son has eaten it two or three times a week since he was three years old—that's a lot of cauliflower! To avoid a rut, I've added various flavors over the years, brightening the dish and spicing things up. The truth is, Jivan prefers the tried-and-true classic: EVOO, sea salt, and pepper. But for the grown-ups in my life, I've come up with this parsley, lemon zest, caper, and jalapeño combo. Just toss it with the cauliflower when it comes out of the oven—and don't forget to put some plain florets aside for the little ones.

SERVES 4 TO 6

—

1 head cauliflower, quartered, cored, and cut into bite-size florets

3 to 4 tablespoons extra-virgin olive oil, plus extra for drizzling

Salt and freshly cracked pepper

1 lemon

1 large handful fresh parsley (about ½ cup/25 g), roughly chopped

1 tablespoon capers

1 jalapeño chile, seeded and thinly sliced

Flaky sea salt, for serving

Preheat the oven to 425°F (220°C). Spread the cauliflower on a baking sheet in a single layer. Drizzle with the oil, season generously with salt and pepper, and toss to coat. Roast the cauliflower, tossing the florets halfway through, until they are deep golden and crispy, 30 to 35 minutes total.

While the cauliflower is roasting, use a vegetable peeler to peel 3 strips of zest from the lemon. Cut each strip crosswise into very thin slices. Cut the lemon in half, reserving one half and storing the other for another use.

Transfer the roasted cauliflower to a serving bowl. Top it with the parsley, capers, jalapeño, and sliced lemon zest. Squeeze the mixture with the lemon half and drizzle it with more oil. Toss to coat all of the ingredients, and sprinkle with a pinch or two of the flaky salt.

Heads of cauliflower vary greatly in size. If you buy a large one and find that your florets don't fit easily in a single layer on one baking sheet, use two sheets. A mound of veg will end up soggy and steamy rather than beautifully browned.

MISO-GLAZED CARROTS
WITH CARROT-TOP PESTO

Growing up, I refused to eat anything I considered an "exotic" food. It wasn't until I moved to New York City in the late nineties and starting working at Indochine—the iconic Asian-fusion eatery in Soho—that I finally broadened my horizons. In fact, I fell so hard for the restaurant's cuisine that when I first started cooking, I stuck almost exclusively to an Asian flavor profile: miso, ginger, and sesame were my mainstays. I used them so much that I eventually got a bit tired of them—except when it comes to carrots. I love pan-roasting those sweet little roots, and the combination of miso and butter transforms them into something truly amazing. My old friends ginger and sesame come into the picture in the form of a carrot-top pesto. Yes, carrot tops! Those lacy greens you normally toss are actually edible. Bitter and earthy, they're just the right balance for zippy ginger and nutty seeds.

SERVES 4

—

FOR THE PESTO

1 bunch leafy carrot tops, very finely chopped

1 large handful fresh parsley, very finely chopped

2 green onions, thinly sliced

1 clove garlic, minced

½ teaspoon minced fresh ginger

1 lime, zested and juiced

2 tablespoons pumpkin seeds, toasted and roughly chopped, plus more for garnish

2 teaspoons sesame seeds, toasted

⅓ cup (75 ml) extra-virgin olive oil

Salt and freshly cracked pepper

FOR THE CARROTS

2 tablespoons white miso paste

2 tablespoons unsalted butter

1 tablespoon light brown sugar

2 tablespoons grapeseed oil

1½ pounds (680 g) small to medium carrots, peeled and halved lengthwise

Aleppo pepper, for serving

Make the pesto: In a medium bowl, mix together the carrot tops, parsley, onions, garlic, ginger, lime zest, lime juice, pumpkin seeds, and sesame seeds. Add the olive oil and stir to combine. Season with salt and pepper and set aside.

Make the carrots: In a small bowl, mix together the miso, butter, and sugar. In a large, heavy-bottomed skillet, heat the grapeseed oil over medium-high heat. Working in two batches, add half the carrots and cook, stirring occasionally, until they are browned and fork tender. Transfer the carrots to a plate and repeat with the remaining batch. After all the carrots are cooked, return them to the skillet and lower the heat. Add the miso mixture and cook, tossing to coat, until the carrots are glossy, 2 minutes. Season to taste with salt and pepper. Serve the carrots warm, topped with pesto. Finish with a sprinkle of pumpkin seeds and a pinch of Aleppo pepper. Serve additional pesto on the side.

Pretty little dishes are like jewelry for the table: small touches that make a big difference in the overall look. I use them for serving sauce, as well as for salt and pepper—especially the vibrantly crimson flakes of Aleppo seen here. Bonus points for a dainty golden spoon.

CHARRED BROCCOLINI
WITH GREEN RELISH AND FETA

We eat two or three heads of broccoli a week in my house, much of it as a pre-dinner nibble that I set out on the kitchen island while I prep the rest of our meal. That broccoli, which we always eat with our fingers, is simply blanched and sprinkled with olive oil and sea salt—not really recipe worthy, but delicious. (You should try it!) But this version, which is roasted to a crisp in the oven and then tossed with a sweet-spicy green onion relish, is really something special. Creamy feta and spiced chickpeas make delicious additions, but they're certainly not essential to the recipe.

SERVES 4

—

FOR THE RELISH

1 small clove garlic, minced

½ teaspoon kosher salt

1 jalapeño, minced (seeds removed if you are heat sensitive)

3 green onions, white and pale green parts only, thinly sliced into rounds

2 limes, zested and juiced

2 teaspoons honey

1 tablespoon extra-virgin olive oil

2 teaspoons chopped fresh cilantro

FOR THE BROCCOLINI

3 heads broccolini (about 1½ pounds/680 g), trimmed and split vertically into florets

3 tablespoons extra-virgin olive oil

Salt and freshly cracked pepper

4 ounces (115 g) feta, crumbled

2 tablespoons Spiced Chickpeas (page 270)

Aleppo pepper or red pepper flakes, for serving (optional)

Make the relish: Preheat the oven to 425°F (220°C). On a cutting board, use the back of a chef's knife to mash together the garlic and salt into a paste. Transfer the paste to a medium bowl and combine it with the jalapeño, onions, lime zest and juice, honey, oil, and the cilantro.

Make the broccolini: Spread the broccolini on a baking sheet and drizzle it with the oil. Season with salt and pepper and gently toss until it's all evenly coated. Roast the broccolini until it is slightly crispy and charred on the edges, 20 to 25 minutes.

To serve, toss the broccolini with the relish and spread it on a platter; finish with the feta and spiced chickpeas. Sprinkle with Aleppo pepper, if using.

Broccolini's delicate shape sets it apart from basic bushy varieties. Show off that leggy silhouette by slicing it vertically and serving it on a platter rather than piling it into a bowl.

WILD MUSHROOM RISOTTO

When I took my first cooking lesson, while I was pregnant with Jivan, risotto was the very first dish I learned to make. So when I hosted my first holiday dinner, you can guess what I served! My affection for the creamy Italian rice was reaffirmed two years ago, when I had the opportunity to collaborate with Jody Williams, the chef-owner of New York's Buvette and Via Carota, on a harvest dinner at Westwind Orchard. We made the two-hour trip upstate for a site visit, and left the farm so invigorated by the autumn bounty that we had the entire menu finalized by the time we got back to the city. One of the dishes Jody created was risotto with wild mushrooms and wild berries—the inspiration being the edible treasures you'd find on the forest floor. The idea was so poetic that I couldn't help trying to create my own interpretation. As written, it's an early fall recipe, since it relies on wild berries, but it can also be made later in the season; just omit the fruit.

SERVES 4

—

4½ cups (1 L) low-sodium chicken
  stock

5 tablespoons (2½ ounces/70 g)
  unsalted butter, divided

2 cloves garlic, minced

2 large shallots, finely chopped

12 ounces (340 g) fresh wild
  mushrooms such as chanterelles and
  hedgehogs, trimmed and halved, the
  larger pieces roughly chopped

5 fresh sage leaves, finely chopped

3 sprigs fresh rosemary, leaves minced

4 sprigs fresh thyme

Salt and freshly cracked pepper

1½ cups (285 g) Arborio rice

¾ cup (180 ml) dry white wine

3 tablespoons mascarpone

¾ cup (70 g) finely grated Parmigiano-
  Reggiano, plus more for serving

1 handful (about ¾ cup) wild black
  currants or blackberries, for serving

1 teaspoon chopped fresh chives and/
  or parsley

1 lemon, zested

In a medium saucepan, bring the stock to a simmer over medium heat and keep it at a bare simmer, covered.

In a heavy saucepan, melt 4 tablespoons (2 ounces/55 g) of the butter over medium-high heat. Add the garlic and shallots and sauté until softened, 1 to 2 minutes. Add the mushrooms and herbs, stirring occasionally, until the mushrooms are softened and just turning golden brown and their liquid has evaporated, 5 to 7 minutes. Season with salt and pepper.

Add the rice and cook, stirring, until it turns opaque, about 1 minute. Add the wine and cook until it has almost evaporated. Using a ladle, add 1 cup (240 ml) of the hot stock and simmer, stirring, until it has fully evaporated. Continue to add the stock, about ½ cup (120 ml) at a time, stirring frequently and allowing each addition to be fully absorbed by the rice before adding the next. When the rice is just tender and creamy looking, in 20 to 25 minutes, it is done; it should be cooked through but still have a slight bite to it.

Remove the risotto from the heat and discard the thyme stems. Stir in the remaining 1 tablespoon butter, the mascarpone, and Parmigiano-Reggiano, and season to taste with salt and pepper. If the risotto is thicker than you'd like it to be, you can thin it with some of the leftover stock.

Just before serving the risotto, garnish it with the wild berries, chives, a few shaves of Parmigiano-Reggiano, and the lemon zest. Adjust the seasoning to taste. Serve immediately.

Hand-thrown ceramics are, by their nature, one of a kind, so don't feel pressure to invest in an entire set of any one style. Here, I've used three different shapes, pulled together by a shared neutral palette.

ORECCHIETTE WITH KALE, FENNEL, AND SAUSAGE

This recipe came about by happy accident on a day when my market was out of just about everything on my shopping list. I picked up a few links of pork sausage and a bunch of lacinato kale and headed home without any real plan. In the fridge, I found a bulb of fennel and thought, why not? The flavors ended up melding so deliciously that it's been a weeknight standard ever since. As yummy as it is, this is one of those recipes that should be used as a guide rather than taken as gospel. Have fun with it and adapt it to suit your needs. Omit the pasta, add more broth, and you have soup. Get rid of the sausage and it's a great vegetarian dish. Play around with what you've got—it's how all the best recipes are born.

SERVES 4

—

¼ cup (60 ml) extra-virgin olive oil

1½ pounds (680 g) fresh Italian pork sausage, removed from their casings (I prefer a half-and-half mix of sweet and spicy)

4 cloves garlic, smashed and chopped

1 shallot, thinly sliced

1 teaspoon red pepper flakes (optional)

1 fennel bulb, cored, quartered, and thinly sliced

½ teaspoon kosher salt, plus more for seasoning

⅔ cup (165 ml) chicken stock

1 bunch lacinato kale, ribs removed and roughly chopped

1 pound (455 g) dried orecchiette pasta

Grated Parmigiano-Reggiano cheese, for serving

Freshly cracked pepper, for serving

In a large skillet, heat the oil over medium-high heat. Add the sausage and cook, stirring and breaking up the meat, until it's browned on all sides, 7 to 10 minutes. Remove the sausage with a slotted spoon and transfer it to a plate.

Add the garlic to the same skillet and sauté for 2 minutes, until light golden. Add the shallot and cook for 2 minutes more. Add the red pepper flakes, if using, and cook until fragrant, about 30 seconds. Add the fennel and salt and sauté until the fennel has softened, 3 to 5 minutes. Add the stock and cook a few minutes more.

Bring a large pot of salted water to a boil over high heat. Add the kale to the boiling water and blanch it for 2 to 3 minutes. Using a slotted spoon, remove the kale and add it to the skillet, along with the sausage. Return the water to a boil and add the pasta. Cook according to the package directions until al dente.

Drain the pasta into a colander, making sure to reserve 1 cup (240 ml) of the cooking water. Add the pasta to the skillet and cook it with the sausage and kale over low heat for 1 to 2 minutes. If the pasta is dry, moisten it with the reserved pasta water, adding ¼ cup (60 ml) at a time. Check and adjust the seasoning.

Finish the pasta with grated cheese and freshly cracked pepper. Serve immediately.

I don't turn up my nose at the high-quality pre-grated Parm that's now available at many markets, but there are times when it's worth it to buy a wedge of cheese and pull out your Microplane—and this is one of them. Snowy, hand-grated wisps of cheese add a wonderfully ethereal touch to this hearty pasta.

SLOW-ROASTED ARCTIC CHAR WITH CRANBERRY CHUTNEY

One of my all-time favorite fall outings is visiting the cranberry bog that's just a few miles from our home in Amagansett. To get there we stroll down the Walking Dunes Trail and through an otherworldly area known as the Phantom Forest, where thirty-foot trees are almost entirely covered by shifting sand. Every year, just before Thanksgiving, we gather as many wild berries as we can carry. While I love them in desserts, this savory chutney might just be my favorite cranberry concoction. The jewel-toned fruit teams up with thyme, shallots, and preserved lemons to create a puckeringly tart counterbalance to creamy acorn squash and rich Arctic char. Hearty and full of fall flavors, it's a perfect pescatarian option for Thanksgiving.

SERVES 4
—

FOR THE ARCTIC CHAR

1 acorn squash, halved and cut into 1-inch-thick (2.5-cm-thick) half moons

Extra-virgin olive oil, for drizzling

Salt and freshly cracked pepper

1 whole Arctic char fillet (about 1½ pounds/680 g)

1 orange, zested; ½ juiced

A few sprigs fresh thyme, some leaves reserved for serving

2 tablespoons pepitas, toasted, reserved for serving

FOR THE CHUTNEY

2 tablespoons extra-virgin olive oil

1 clove garlic, chopped

1 shallot, finely chopped

A few sprigs fresh thyme, leaves removed and roughly chopped

1 teaspoon minced habanero chile

2 cups (190 g) whole cranberries (if fresh are unavailable, substitute frozen)

¾ cup (180 ml) fresh orange juice, divided, plus more if needed

3 tablespoons turbinado sugar

1 tablespoon orange zest

1 preserved lemon (store-bought, or see recipe on page 269), rind finely chopped, a handful reserved for garnish

Make the char: Preheat the oven to 425°F (220°C). Spread the squash on a baking sheet; drizzle it with oil and season with salt and pepper. Roast the squash until golden and crisp on one side, about 15 minutes. Using a spatula, flip the squash and cook for another 5 minutes. Reduce the heat to 325°F (165°C).

Remove the squash from the oven and push it to the perimeter of the baking sheet. Place the Arctic char on the baking sheet; sprinkle it with the orange juice and half of the orange zest. Drizzle the fish lightly with oil, scatter with the thyme sprigs, and season with salt and pepper. Roast until the fish is cooked through, about 20 minutes.

Make the chutney: In a medium saucepan, heat the oil over medium heat. Add the garlic and shallot and sauté until soft and translucent. Add the thyme and chile; sauté for 1 minute. Stir in the cranberries, ½ cup (120 ml) of the orange juice, and the sugar. Simmer, stirring occasionally, until the cranberries have burst and the sauce has reduced, 6 to 8 minutes (if your cranberries are frozen, this will take 8 to 10 minutes). Stir in the orange zest, lemon rind, and remaining ¼ cup (60 ml) orange juice. If the chutney seems too thick, thin it with additional juice.

Just before serving, garnish the fish with the reserved lemon rind, reserved orange zest, toasted pepitas, and a handful of thyme leaves. Serve the cranberry chutney on the side.

Flavorwise, the cranberry chutney and Arctic char are a perfect match. Visually, however, they don't play well together on a platter—the jammy sauce, spooned over the fish, can look sloppy. In the interest of pretty presentation, serve the chutney on the side.

SEARED BLACK BASS
WITH SMASHED POTATOES AND BLACK OLIVES

With briny olives, crispy-creamy potatoes, and full-flavored herbs, this is a hearty fish dish perfectly suited to late fall. The true star is the warm vinaigrette, which boasts a punchy vibrant tang. Serve extra on the side; you will want it with every bite! Here, I've used black bass, but any firm, white, delicately flavored fish will suffice. Try striped bass, sea bass, snapper, branzino, or even flounder. And while I haven't included it in the recipe, I sometimes serve the fish with a dollop of crème fraîche or full-fat Greek yogurt.

SERVES 4

—

1½ pounds (680 g) baby Yukon Gold potatoes

4 tablespoons (60 ml) extra-virgin olive oil, divided, plus more for drizzling

Salt and freshly cracked pepper

4 cloves garlic, thinly sliced

⅔ cup (105 g) pitted kalamata olives, roughly chopped

3 sprigs fresh oregano, leaves chopped, plus more for garnish

2 sprigs fresh rosemary, leaves chopped

½ cup (120 ml) fresh lemon juice

4 skin-on black bass fillets (about 6 ounces/170 g each), patted dry

Preheat the oven to 400°F (205°C).

Place the potatoes in a pot of salted water and bring to a simmer over medium heat. Cook until the potatoes are tender but retain their shape, about 10 minutes. Drain the potatoes into a colander.

Spread the potatoes on a parchment-lined baking sheet. Using a flat-bottomed cup or mug, gently smash the potatoes, then drizzle them generously with oil and season with salt and pepper. Roast the potatoes, flipping them with a spatula halfway through, until golden and crispy, 20 to 25 minutes.

Meanwhile, in a small skillet, heat 2 tablespoons of the oil over medium heat. Add the garlic and sauté until soft and lightly golden, about 1 minute (be careful here: The garlic can burn in a split second). Add the olives and sauté for 1 minute, then add the herbs and sauté for 1 minute more. Add the lemon juice and simmer for a few minutes until slightly reduced. Stir in the remaining 2 tablespoons oil and season with salt and pepper. Set the skillet aside and keep the vinaigrette warm.

Season the bass fillets with salt and pepper. In a heavy-bottomed skillet, heat a splash of oil over medium-high heat. Place the fillets in the skillet skin-side down. Sear until the skin is golden and crispy, about 5 minutes. Flip the fillets and cook until just cooked through, 2 to 3 minutes more.

To serve, spoon the warm vinaigrette over the fillets and smashed potatoes. Garnish with oregano and serve immediately.

To get beautifully crisp skin on your fish, give the fillets a good pat with a paper towel before cooking so they don't steam on the heat. (Steam is the enemy of browning.) And resist the urge to flip or otherwise mess with the fish until the edges naturally release from the pan. Patience pays!

SWORDFISH WITH RAISINS AND ROASTED LEMON-OLIVE CHUTNEY

Olives, lemons, and raisins might sound like an odd combination, but it's actually a classic Sicilian flavor profile. And really good things come from Sicily—like my mother-in-law! (Giovanna, this one's for you.) The sweet raisins, salty olives, and sour charred lemons are particularly delicious spooned over swordfish, their lively flavors counterbalancing the hearty, buttery fish. All that's missing? A little crunch, which comes from a sprinkling of Marcona almonds just before serving.

SERVES 4

—

FOR THE CHUTNEY

⅓ cup (50 g) golden raisins

⅓ cup (75 ml) white wine vinegar

2 lemons, cut into ¼-inch-thick (6-mm-thick) rounds, ends and seeds discarded

⅔ cup (165 ml) extra-virgin olive oil, plus extra for drizzling

½ cup (75 g) Castelvetrano olives, roughly chopped

2 or 3 cloves garlic, minced

2 tablespoons chopped fresh parsley

2 tablespoons fresh lemon juice

2 teaspoons honey

¾ teaspoon kosher salt

Freshly cracked pepper

FOR THE SWORDFISH

2 (12-ounce/340-g) swordfish steaks, about 1 inch (2.5 cm) thick

Salt and freshly cracked pepper

Extra-virgin olive oil, for drizzling

¼ cup (35 g) salted Marcona almonds, roughly chopped

A few sprigs fresh parsley, for serving

Make the chutney: Preheat the oven to broil.

Place the raisins in a small bowl. In a small saucepan, heat the vinegar over medium heat until steaming. Pour the vinegar over the raisins and soak until they are plump, 10 to 15 minutes. Drain, discarding the vinegar.

In a bowl, toss the lemon rounds with a drizzle of oil until evenly coated. Spread the lemons on a baking sheet in a single layer and broil on high until slightly charred, 7 to 8 minutes. Let them cool slightly, then chop the lemons into small pieces. Transfer them to a bowl and stir together with the oil, raisins, olives, garlic, parsley, lemon juice, honey, and salt. Season with freshly cracked pepper.

Make the swordfish: Heat a cast-iron skillet or grill over medium-high heat until it begins to smoke. Season the fish with salt and pepper. Drizzle the pan with oil and immediately add the fish to the skillet. Cook the fish until golden and cooked through, about 6 minutes per side.

Just before serving, spoon the relish over the swordfish and scatter it with the almonds. Garnish with the parsley and offer extra relish on the side.

Go for the gold! From the raisins to the lemons to the perfectly caramelized fish, this is a delightfully tawny plate of food. Provide a hint of contrast by reserving a few whole, perky sprigs of parsley to sprinkle over the finished dish. A parsley garnish doesn't have to be cliché!

PAN-ROASTED CHICKEN
WITH SHALLOTS AND DATES

This is, hands down, the most requested meal in my house—and that's really saying something when you consider the fact that, prior to tasting it, Victor never liked chicken on the bone and Jivan would not touch a shallot. Once you try it, you won't be surprised that I made believers out of both of them—it's the yummiest bird you'll ever feast on. I do owe some of the credit to my cast-iron skillet. It retains heat evenly, is practically nonstick when seasoned, and transfers from the stovetop to the oven with ease—in other words, it's perfect for pan-roasting. Thanks to this technique, the finished bird has a crunchy golden skin and is bursting with juice. Adding to the deliciousness are melt-in-your-mouth shallots and a sweet, tart, buttery pan sauce.

SERVES 4

—

4 bone-in, skin-on chicken breast
 halves

Salt and freshly cracked pepper

2 tablespoons grapeseed oil

4 tablespoons (2 ounces/55 g)
 unsalted butter, divided

10 shallots, peeled, larger ones halved
 lengthwise

4 cloves garlic, smashed and roughly
 chopped

8 to 10 sprigs fresh thyme, divided

½ cup (120 ml) dry white wine

1½ cups (360 ml) low-sodium
 chicken stock

8 Medjool dates, pitted and halved
 lengthwise

⅔ cup (105 g) green olives, smashed
 and pitted

1½ tablespoons apple cider vinegar

1 lemon, zested and juiced

Set the chicken out at room temperature for 30 minutes before cooking.

Preheat the oven to 450°F (230°C). Position a rack in the top third of your oven.

Place your largest cast-iron skillet in the oven for 15 minutes. Pat the chicken breasts dry and generously season them on all sides with salt and pepper. Carefully remove the hot skillet from the oven and place it on the stovetop. Add the grapeseed oil to the skillet and heat it over medium-high heat until the oil has a subtle ripple effect. You want the oil to be very hot. Working in two batches, cook the chicken, skin-side down, until the skin is crispy and golden brown, 4 to 5 minutes. Drain off all but 1 tablespoon of oil from the pan.

Remove the chicken from the skillet and set it onto a plate as you build your sauce. Over medium heat, melt 2 tablespoons of the butter in the skillet and add the shallots. Cook the shallots undisturbed for 5 to 6 minutes, until they are caramelized and golden. Add the garlic, a few thyme sprigs, 1 tablespoon of the butter, and season with salt and pepper. Toss the shallots and continue to cook until they begin to soften, 5 to 7 minutes. Deglaze the pan with the wine and reduce it by half. Add a few more thyme sprigs and the stock. Simmer the sauce over medium to low heat for 15 minutes, until reduced slightly. Check for seasoning and add the dates and olives to the sauce.

Return the chicken breasts to the skillet, skin-side up, and place it in the oven. Roast the chicken until it's just cooked through, about 20 minutes. An instant-read thermometer inserted in the thickest part of the breast should register 160°F (70°C).

Transfer the chicken breasts to a plate; set them aside and keep warm. Return the skillet to the stovetop over medium to low heat and add the vinegar to the sauce. Simmer until the sauce is thick enough to coat the back of a wooden spoon, 3 to 5 minutes. Remove it from the heat and stir in the remaining 1 tablespoon butter and the lemon juice. Check and adjust the seasoning. Return the chicken to the skillet and serve it immediately, garnished with the remaining thyme and the lemon zest.

One of the first things you learn at cooking school is to drape a dish cloth over the handle of a hot pan as a warning that it's scalding. If you're bringing the pan to the table, be sure to use your prettiest tea towel.

ONE-POT STEWED PORK WITH BUTTERNUT SQUASH AND WALNUT GREMOLATA

There's nothing quite as cozy as the smell of a braise bubbling in the oven on a lazy Sunday afternoon. And in my opinion, pork shoulder is the braise to end all braises—it falls apart naturally as it cooks, shredding into the perfect texture. As you might have noticed by now, I love to top my proteins with crunchy, bright finishing sauces, and this gremolata is particularly crunchy and bright. The pomegranates, walnuts, and orange lend a refreshingly vibrant bite to the richly developed flavors of the pork.

SERVES 6
—
FOR THE STEW

6 cups (690 g) peeled and cubed butternut squash

1 tablespoon extra-virgin olive oil, plus extra for drizzling

1 tablespoon honey

2 teaspoons minced habanero chile, divided

Salt and freshly cracked pepper

2 teaspoons canola oil

4 pounds (1.8 kg) boneless pork shoulder

4 cloves garlic, chopped

2 onions, chopped

4 carrots, peeled, halved lengthwise, and chopped

4 stalks celery, diced

⅔ cup (165 ml) dry sherry

2 bay leaves

1 bunch fresh sage (1 or 2 sprigs reserved for garnish, leaves chopped)

1 head garlic, halved

6 cups (1.4 L) low-sodium chicken stock

2 tablespoons apple cider vinegar

FOR THE GREMOLATA

¾ cup (65 g) pomegranate seeds

¾ cup (75 g) walnuts, toasted and chopped

⅓ cup (17 g) fresh parsley

3 tablespoons fresh chopped chives

3 tablespoons finely diced shallot

1 orange, zested, plus 3 tablespoons juice

Salt and freshly cracked pepper

Make the stew: Preheat the oven to 425°F (220°C). Place the squash on a baking sheet and drizzle it with the olive oil and honey. Sprinkle the squash with 1 teaspoon of the habanero, then season with salt and pepper. Toss to evenly coat the squash, then spread in a single layer. Roast, tossing halfway through, until golden and crispy, about 30 minutes. Remove from the oven and let sit at room temperature until ready to use. Lower the oven to 325°F (165°C).

While the squash is roasting, heat the canola oil in a large Dutch oven over medium-high heat. Trim any excess fat from the pork, pat it dry, and season it very generously with salt and pepper. Sear until it's well browned on all sides, 20 to 25 minutes total. Transfer the pork to a plate and set aside.

Lower the heat and add the 1 tablespoon olive oil, chopped garlic, onion, and remaining 1 teaspoon habanero. Sauté until the onions are soft and translucent, 3 to 5 minutes. Add the carrots and celery and sauté until they begin to soften, about 5 minutes. Add the sherry and use it to deglaze any browned bits that are sticking to the bottom of the pot. When the sherry has reduced by about half, add the bay leaves, sage, and halved garlic head. Add the stock and bring it to a simmer. Return the pork to the pot. Crumple and wet a piece of parchment paper and place it directly on top of the braise. Cover the pot with a tight-fitting lid and place it in the oven. Cook until the pork is very tender, about 4 hours.

Make the gremolata: Toss all of the ingredients together until well combined, then season with salt and pepper.

When the pork has finished cooking, remove and discard the parchment paper. Transfer the pork to a large plate. Remove and discard the sage, bay leaves, and halved garlic head. Return the pot to the stovetop and simmer the cooking liquid for 5 minutes. Add the vinegar and simmer until the liquid has thickened slightly, about 5 minutes more. Remove from the heat, cover, and keep warm.

Break the pork into large pieces, discarding any large pieces of fat. Return the pork to the pot, then add the roasted squash and toss gently to combine. Taste for seasoning.

Serve the braised pork with a generous spoonful of gremolata and a pinch of chopped sage.

Stewed pork is beyond delicious, but let's face it: A big bowl of shredded meat isn't going to win any beauty pageants. Draw the eye to one of the more picturesque elements of the dish—the bright orange butternut—with a napkin that picks up its autumnal hue.

HANGER STEAK WITH CARAMELIZED ENDIVE AND ROASTED GARLIC MASHED POTATOES

The Calderones are carnivores, through and through, and hanger steak is one of our favorite meaty mains. The magic is in the marinade, which, like all good marinades, follows a classic formula. You need acid to tenderize, an aromatic such as garlic or shallot to add flavor, a salty component to help lock in moisture, a little something sweet to assist in browning, and some herbs for brightness. Here, balsamic, Dijon, garlic, and rosemary do the trick.

SERVES 4

—

FOR THE STEAK

2 sprigs fresh rosemary, leaves finely
  chopped

½ cup (120 ml) extra-virgin olive oil

4 cloves garlic, minced

3 tablespoons balsamic vinegar

2 tablespoons Dijon mustard

1 lemon, zested

Small pinch minced habanero chile
  (optional)

Kosher salt

2 pounds (910 g) hanger steak

2 teaspoons canola or grapeseed oil

Thyme leaves, for serving

Flaky sea salt and freshly cracked
  pepper, for serving

FOR THE ENDIVE

3 tablespoons unsalted butter

4 teaspoons sugar

Fresh thyme sprigs

4 large Belgian endives, sliced in half
  from tip to root

Salt and freshly cracked pepper

FOR THE POTATOES

1 head garlic

Extra-virgin olive oil, for drizzling

2½ pounds (1.2 kg) Yukon Gold
  potatoes, peeled and quartered

¾ stick (3 ounces/85 g) butter

¾ cup (180 ml) half-and-half

Salt and freshly cracked pepper

Make the marinade: In a small bowl, combine the rosemary, olive oil, garlic, vinegar, mustard, lemon zest, chile (if using), and 1 teaspoon of salt. Cover the steaks with the marinade and refrigerate them for 1 to 2 hours or overnight.

Make the endive: In a large skillet over high heat, melt the butter and stir in the sugar and thyme sprigs. When the mixture begins to bubble, place the endive in the pan cut-side down. Cook until the bottoms of the endive are caramelized, 3 to 5 minutes.

Line a baking sheet with parchment paper and transfer the endive to the parchment, cut-sides up. Season the top of the endive with salt and pepper. Roast until caramelized and golden, 10 to 12 minutes. Remove and set aside at room temperature until ready to use.

Make the potatoes: Preheat the oven to 400°F (205°C). Slice off the very top of the garlic head, then drizzle it with oil and wrap it in foil. Place it on a baking sheet and cook until the garlic is tender and fragrant, about 35 minutes. Remove the garlic from the oven and let it cool until it can be handled comfortably. Leave the oven on. Remove the cloves and mash them with a wooden spoon.

Remove the steak from the marinade and bring it to room temperature.

Place the potatoes in a large stockpot and cover with cold water. Bring the water to a boil and cook until the potatoes are fork tender, about 20 minutes. Drain and return the potatoes to the pot. Cook them over low heat for a few minutes to remove any excess moisture, then add the roasted garlic, butter, and half-and-half. Using a wooden spoon, mash everything together until the potatoes are smooth but chunky. Season with salt and pepper. Set aside and keep warm.

Make the steak: Dry the steak with a paper towel, blotting away any remaining marinade or moisture. Season the steak with salt on both sides. Heat the oil in a cast-iron skillet over high heat. When the skillet is smoking hot, cook the steak for 4 minutes on each side for medium-rare. Allow it to rest for 5 minutes, then slice it against the grain and serve immediately.

Divide the mashed potatoes between each plate with slices of steak and a few pieces of caramelized endive. Garnish with thyme and season with flaky sea salt and freshly cracked pepper. Serve immediately.

swoon tip

To get a deep brown sear on your steak, avoid crowding the pan. Crowding decreases the temperature of the skillet, which makes it hard to get that coveted color and crust without overcooking.

CARDAMOM-COGNAC APPLE CAKE

Without fail, as soon as the weather gets crisp, I get the urge to head upstate on an apple-picking adventure. And, also without fail, I end up with an enormous, overflowing bushel of fruit—way more than my little family could ever eat out of hand! One of my favorite ways to make use of them is this classic French apple cake. I started off making a traditional recipe years ago, but have been experimenting with it pretty much ever since. The result is a moist, bread pudding–like cake—thanks to the addition of buttermilk—that tastes deliciously decadent but not too sweet. Cognac and cardamom add a little something special, but don't overwhelm the bright, clean apple taste.

SERVES 8 TO 10
—

1 cup (125 g) all-purpose flour

¾ teaspoon ground cardamom

¾ teaspoon baking powder

¼ teaspoon kosher salt

2 large eggs, at room temperature

¾ cup (150 g) granulated sugar

3 tablespoons cognac (Calvados, rum, or bourbon work well, too)

½ teaspoon vanilla extract

⅓ cup (75 ml) well-shaken buttermilk, at room temperature

3 medium Honeycrisp apples

1 stick (4 ounces/115 g) unsalted butter, melted and cooled, plus more for greasing the pan

1 tablespoon turbinado sugar

Confectioners' sugar, for dusting

Preheat the oven to 350°F (175°C). Nestle a piece of parchment paper into an 8- or 9-inch (20- or 23-cm) cast-iron pan and grease it with butter.

In a bowl, whisk together the flour, cardamom, baking powder, and salt. In a separate large bowl, beat the eggs until foamy. Whisk in the granulated sugar, cognac, and vanilla extract. Pour in the buttermilk and whisk to combine.

Peel, halve, and core 2½ of the apples, then cut them into ½-inch-thick (12-mm-thick) cubes. Reserve the remaining half apple, unpeeled, and cut it into ¼-inch (6-mm) slices, for the top.

Add half of the flour mixture to the wet ingredients, stirring until just combined, then gently fold in half of the melted butter. Repeat with the remaining flour mixture and melted butter. Gently fold in the cubed apples, reserving the slices. Transfer the batter to the pan and arrange the apples slices in a circular pattern on top of the batter. Sprinkle with the turbinado sugar. Bake until the cake turns a deep golden brown and a cake tester inserted in the center comes out clean, 55 to 65 minutes. Transfer the skillet to a cooling rack and let it sit for 5 minutes. The cake may be served warm or at room temperature, directly from the skillet; whichever you choose, make sure to dust it with confectioners' sugar before serving.

swoon tip I love the rustic presentation of baking—and serving—this cake in a cast-iron skillet. A ruffled layer of parchment paper not only adds to the homey feel, it makes for an easy release. And don't skimp when sprinkling raw sugar over the apples. It's the key to their deep caramel hue.

PEAR AND HAZELNUT TART

The very first "from scratch" dessert that I mastered was a proper French pear tart. Still a nervous cook, I was petrified at the idea of rolling out classic pastry dough, so, after much research, I found a recipe with a pressed-in crust—one that goes straight from mixing bowl to pan, where it's smushed into shape with your fingers. Though I chose to make the tart because it was easy, I was blown away by its flavors—and by the oohs and aaahs of my dinner party guests. This recipe is an adaption of that original dessert, modernized with an almond- and hazelnut-infused crust and a lavender honey and crème fraîche filling.

SERVES 6 TO 8

—

FOR THE CRUST

1 stick (4 ounces/115 g) unsalted
  butter, melted and cooled, plus more
  for greasing the pan

½ cup (100 g) sugar

½ teaspoon fine sea salt

¼ teaspoon almond extract

¼ teaspoon vanilla extract

1¼ cups (155 g) all-purpose flour

3 tablespoons hazelnut flour

FOR THE FILLING

½ cup (120 ml) crème fraîche

1 large egg, lightly beaten

2 tablespoons honey

1 teaspoon pure vanilla extract

¼ teaspoon pure almond extract

1 tablespoon Wondra flour or sifted
  all-purpose flour

2 teaspoons hazelnut flour

2 ripe but firm Bosc pears, peeled,
  halved, cored, and thinly sliced

Semisweet chocolate shavings, for
  garnish

⅓ cup (45 g) hazelnuts, toasted and
  roughly chopped, for garnish

Confectioners' sugar, for dusting

Make the crust: Preheat the oven to 350°F (175°C). Butter a 13¾ by 4½-inch (35 by 11-cm) rectangular fluted tart pan with a removable bottom; a 9-inch (23-cm) round tart pan with a removable bottom will also work.

In a medium bowl, whisk together the melted butter, sugar, salt, and both extracts. Add flours and stir until well combined; you should end up with a soft, pliable dough. Press the dough evenly over the bottom and sides of the pan, creating a thin layer; make sure to press the dough firmly into the corners of the pan and seal up any cracks. Lightly prick the dough all over with a fork. Place the pan on a baking sheet and bake until the crust has turned golden brown, about 15 minutes. Transfer the tart pan to a wire rack and let it cool completely.

Make the filling: In a medium bowl, whisk together the crème fraîche, egg, honey, and extracts. Add both flours and stir until they are fully incorporated. When the filling is smooth, pour it into the crust; arrange the pear slices on top of the filling. Bake for 30 to 35 minutes, or until the filling is set and the fruit is tender. Transfer the tart to the wire rack and let it cool slightly before releasing from pan.

Just before you serve the tart, garnish it with chocolate shavings and the hazelnuts and a dusting of confectioners' sugar. You can serve it warm or at room temperature; it's equally delicious either way.

The elegantly elongated silhouette of this tart provides the perfect backdrop for a curving cascade of fruit. When nestling the slices into the custard, let the pear's graceful, tear-drop shape be your guide. Choose ripe but firm pears for clean, precise slices. And to achieve those delicate coils of shaved chocolate, look no further than your vegetable peeler.

CARROT CAKE TRIFLES
WITH MASCARPONE CRÈME AND PECANS

Baking is very much a creative outlet for me, and half the fun has always been in the research. I love comparing classic recipes and gathering bits and bobs of information to develop my own. In fact, I love it so much that I never make the same Thanksgiving dessert twice. Last November, it was a bunch of Technicolor rainbow carrots that sparked my imagination. After plenty of debating and dreaming, I decided to transform them into carrot cake trifle—and the result was off-the-chain delish. The super-tasty ginger-sherry syrup makes the cake ultra-moist; tangy mascarpone cheese gives the cream real depth; and the candy-coated pecans add amazing crunch. Yes, there are several components involved, but every one of them can be prepared in advance.

MAKES EIGHT,
8- TO 10-OUNCE SERVINGS
—

FOR THE CAKE
Unsalted butter, for greasing the pans
2 cups (250 g) all-purpose flour, plus
   more for the pan
2 teaspoons ground cinnamon
1 teaspoon baking powder
¾ teaspoon baking soda
¾ teaspoon kosher salt
½ teaspoon freshly grated nutmeg
¼ teaspoon ground ginger
2 cups (440 g) packed light brown
   sugar
1 teaspoon vanilla extract
4 large eggs, at room temperature
½ cup (120 ml) canola oil
½ cup (120 ml) applesauce
1 pound (455 g) carrots, peeled and
   coarsely grated (about 3 cups/330 g
   lightly packed)

FOR THE SYRUP
¼ cup (50 g) granulated sugar
¼ cup (60 ml) dry sherry
1-inch (2.5-cm) piece fresh ginger,
   peeled and grated on a Microplane

CONTINUED ON PAGE 197

Make the cake: Preheat the oven to 375°F (190°C). Grease a 9- by 13-inch (23- by 33-cm) baking pan, dust the inside with flour, and tap out the excess.

In a bowl, whisk together the flour, cinnamon, baking powder, baking soda, salt, nutmeg, and ginger.

In the bowl of a stand mixer fitted with the paddle attachment, mix together the brown sugar and vanilla extract on medium speed. Add the eggs one by one, beating well after each addition. Add the oil in a slow, steady stream, then add the applesauce and mix until all of the ingredients are fully combined. Add the dry ingredients in two batches, stirring just until combined—be careful not to overmix. Gently stir in the carrots. Pour the batter into the prepared pan.

Bake until the cake is golden brown and a knife or cake tester inserted into the center comes out clean, 25 to 30 minutes. Transfer the cake to a wire rack and let it cool completely.

Make the syrup: In a saucepan, bring the granulated sugar, sherry, and ¼ cup (60 ml) water to a simmer over medium-high heat. Stir until the sugar has dissolved. Remove from the heat and stir in the ginger. Set aside and let it cool completely.

A trifle is all about layers, but don't worry too much about making them even or precise. Loose dollops of frosting and hand-torn pieces of cake are more inviting than neat and tidy stripes.

FOR THE CANDIED PECANS
½ stick (2 ounces/55 g) butter
2 cups (200 g) pecan halves
3 tablespoons brown sugar
¼ teaspoon kosher salt

FOR THE MASCARPONE CRÈME
14 ounces (400 g) mascarpone
  cheese
½ cup (65 g) confectioners' sugar
1 small lemon, zested and juiced
1 tablespoon vanilla extract
2 cups (480 ml) whipping cream

Make the candied pecans: In a saucepan, brown the butter over medium-high heat. Add the pecans and toss to coat. Add the brown sugar and salt and stir until the sugar evenly coats the pecans and has browned slightly. Spread the pecans on a parchment-lined baking sheet and let them cool completely before roughly chopping.

Make the mascarpone crème: In a medium bowl, whisk together the mascarpone, confectioners' sugar, lemon juice, lemon zest, and vanilla extract. In a separate bowl, whisk the cream at medium speed until stiff peaks form. Using a rubber spatula, gently fold the cream into the mascarpone mixture.

When the cake and syrup have cooled to room temperature, use a cake tester to poke holes all over the top of the cake. Brush the cake liberally with the ginger syrup; you want it to soak through. Break the cake into roughly 1-inch (2.5-cm) pieces.

To layer the trifle, place about 1 inch (2.5 cm) of cake pieces in the bottom of each serving glass. Top with 2 tablespoons of the mascarpone crème and a sprinkle of pecans. Repeat until you've reached the top of the glass, ending with the pecans. If you're not serving the trifles immediately, cover and refrigerate them for up to 2 hours.

THE

FALL

TABLE

In planning the look of my fall harvest dinner at Westwind
Orchard, I didn't have to search far for inspiration. Ripe fruit
filled the apple trees and crimson, golden, and orange leaves
colored the surrounding forest. The stunning setting dictated
everything from the autumnal palette of the flowers to the
warm patina of the copper serving pieces and wood-handled
flatware. Even the smallest touches reflected a sense of rustic
simplicity. Foraged pinecones nestled in the napkins; frayed-
edged linen and basic brown kraft paper adorned the table.
Overhead, twinkling little lights were strung from vintage
orchard ladders—a last-minute design decision that lit up the
gathering in more ways than one.

No.1
BRANCH OUT

Bring fall's natural beauty indoors by displaying a few leafy branches in a simple vase. Don't be fooled into believing they need to be blooming—or even bountiful—to make an impact. In this case, less is more! A minimal arrangement of just two or three stems emphasizes their sculptural silhouettes.

No.2
HARVEST GOLD

Add a warm earthy glow to the table by arranging autumn-hued flowers in a varied collection of amber glass vessels. Check your recycling bin for empty bottles of whiskey, cognac—even kombucha—and peel the labels off with hot water. Sometimes the thriftiest touches can be the most elegant.

No.3
PRETTY LITTLE THINGS

Let fall's rustic vibe inform even the tiniest touches on your table. Use simple leather cord or twine to tie your napkins, tucking in a few foraged elements like pinecones and wheat sprigs for texture. And while place cards can often feel fussy, kraft paper brings them down to earth. Use your prettiest script for a bit of juxtaposition.

No.4
NEUTRAL TERRITORY

While neutral, handmade ceramics are a year-round staple, they look particularly at home on a fall table. And here's a little secret: Many ceramics studios offer pottery with teeny, barely noticeable flaws—pieces known as "seconds"—for a fraction of full price. I'm all about embracing imperfections, so give your local potter a ring!

No.5
HERBAL ESSENCE

In fall, there's almost always a baking sheet of veggies roasting in my oven. Herb-infused olive oil gives them a little extra oomph—and makes a perfect take-home gift for guests. Just add a few sprigs of hearty, full-flavored herbs like rosemary, sage, and thyme to your favorite extra-virgin variety. Clear glass, cork-topped bottles like these are easy to find online.

No.6
FLAME UP

There's nothing more flattering than candlelight and I'm always looking for unexpected ways to bring that flickering warmth to the table. Here, rather than employing a traditional candle holder, I corralled pillars of varying heights on a copper tray, tucking seasonal herbs among them for color.

No.7
POINT BLANC

Fall harvest décor doesn't have to be a ho-hum mix of oranges and browns. A cluster of white and gray pumpkins running down the center of the table looks chic and sophisticated, especially when softened with a few silvery green leaves. I adore a pale, neutral palette—even for my pumpkins!

No.8
GIVE THANKS

Spark meaningful conversations—and add a handmade touch—by printing simple brown paper lunch bags with your favorite quotes about gratitude. Expressing thanks puts a beautiful meal with loved ones in perspective. Guests can read the quotes aloud at the table, and then bring the bags home filled with candied nuts or other sweet treats

No.9
PRETTY PENNY

Pick a hue and carry through! A bunch of disparate tabletop items can feel like a proper collection when united by a single material or tone—in this case, copper. I love the metal's warmth and variety of patinas, especially when paired with fall's earthy palette. To start your own collection, peruse Etsy or eBay.

WINTER

Menu

Kohlrabi Salad
APPLE AND CELERY ROOT WITH BLACK PEPPER YOGURT

Rack of Lamb Roast
FENNEL, ROOT VEGETABLES, AND LEMON CHERMOULA

Blood Orange Bundt Cake
BOURBON BITTER ORANGE GLAZE

THERE'S SOMETHING SERIOUSLY MAGICAL about a winter dinner party. With the lights turned low, candles flickering on the table, and bone-chilling air swirling on the other side of the windowpanes, even the simplest dining space is transformed into a cozy cocoon you never want to leave. Add a rich meal bubbling away on the stove, and you've conjured up my idea of heaven.

I am a homebody, through and through, and winter is a homebody's ideal season. Even in my twenties, when my friends were searching for inspiration and identity in their offices and social circles, I was always happiest feathering my nest. I have always experienced a great sense of pride in creating a beautiful home and cooking delicious meals. And on frigid winter nights when I have little interest in venturing out, I use that inviting space and my lovingly prepared food to lure my friends to me!

I'll never forget that very first dinner party at our apartment in Dumbo. It was February and the whole city felt still, thanks to a fresh blanket of snow on the ground. I invited some friends from yoga and acting class, along with some of Victor's record company crew, and braised a big pot of short ribs, following a classic recipe to the letter. For dessert, I made my very first pastry dough for a pear tart. The feeling I experienced during that dinner—knowing that my guests had happy bellies and full hearts as a result of my careful planning and deeply satisfying work—was truly the starting point of my life in food.

And I still relish that feeling. When the cold weather starts to roll in, I can't resist inviting friends for dinner. These winter feasts tend to be layered and more elaborate than what I serve the rest of the year. We're willing to indulge a bit more on these long, dark nights, to find joy in decadence. And if you're anything like me, you love the planning almost as much as the eating. Should you make pork stew or a hearty ragu? Braised beef or roast lamb? Which bright, crunchy salad would best offset those bold flavors? And how over-the-top can you get with dessert?

My friends tend to gather around the kitchen island while I finish cooking, so I've learned to set out an overflowing cheese board for them to nibble on. At some point, I recruit a few helpers to set the table and light the candles. As soon as we're all seated, the storytelling begins. We indulge in a wine-soaked feast, and then tumble over to the coffee table to have another glass in the glow of the fire.

What I love most is the unapologetic lingering that follows a satisfying meal—everyone is so relaxed, the candles are dripping onto the tablecloth, and we're all aglow from great conversation and a little too much wine. The dirty dishes can wait. No one is rushing off. We're blissfully content in our little cocoon.

IN SEASON

BLOOD ORANGES   KOHLRABI   LENTILS

CARA CARA ORANGES SWEET POTATOES   PERSIMMONS

RADICCHIO   FARRO   PARSNIPS

KUMQUATS   BEETS   POTATOES

KALE   CELERY ROOT

                   GRAPEFRUITS

CHICKPEA-MERGUEZ HASH

Does hash always need to involve potatoes? I say no. To me, a hash is simply a sautéed mish-mash of elements bursting with hearty flavor. Here, I use chickpeas as the base, frying them up with onion, lacinato kale, and slightly spicy merguez sausage. I often make variations of this dish on weekends, throwing in odds and ends from the fridge that I'm looking to use up. It's a very forgiving recipe, and one that doesn't even need to be plated. The fried eggs can be placed right on top of the hash in the skillet, with the runny yolks forming a sauce.

SERVES 4

—

2 teaspoons extra-virgin olive oil

12 ounces (340 g) Merguez sausage, casings removed, broken into pieces

1 yellow onion, thinly sliced

1 clove garlic, minced

1 (15-ounce/400-g) can chickpeas, drained, rinsed, and patted dry with a paper towel

⅛ teaspoon Aleppo pepper

½ bunch lacinato kale, stemmed and thinly sliced (about 1½ cups/100 g)

1 lemon, zested and juiced

4 fried eggs, for serving

Za'atar, for serving (optional)

Flaky sea salt and freshly cracked pepper, for serving

In a 10-inch (25-cm) cast-iron skillet, heat the oil over medium heat. Add the sausage and cook, using a wooden spoon to crumble the meat, until the sausage begins to brown, 4 to 5 minutes. Add the onion and cook, stirring frequently, until soft and translucent, about 4 minutes. Stir in the garlic and cook for 1 minute. Add the chickpeas and Aleppo pepper and cook until the chickpeas are heated through, about 2 minutes. Add the kale and cook just until wilted, 30 seconds. Remove the skillet from the heat and stir in the lemon zest and juice. Taste for seasoning.

Divide the hash between four plates and top each serving with a fried egg, or serve straight from the skillet. Serve sprinkled with za'atar, if desired, flaky sea salt, and freshly cracked pepper.

When it comes to frying eggs, resist the urge to flip. Sunny-side up is so much prettier than a messy over-easy situation. If you're opposed to a runny yolk, simply cover the pan for a minute or two while cooking. The steam will cook the yolk without breaking it.

WHITE BEAN TOASTS WITH RADICCHIO AND LEMON-PARSLEY RELISH

As you've probably gathered by now, olive oil–slathered toast and bright, zesty relish are two of my favorite things on the planet. This irresistible recipe features both, marrying the crunchy bread and citrusy topping with another staple of my kitchen: creamy cannellini beans. What I love most about this particular relish is that it makes use of the entire lemon—peel, pith, and all. The whole fruit is sliced thinly and then chopped with parsley and radicchio, resulting in an earthy, slightly bitter flavor that balances the richness of the garlicky, buttery beans.

MAKES 4 CROSTINI

—

3 teaspoons extra-virgin olive oil, divided, plus more for coating the bread and drizzling

2 cloves garlic, 1 sliced and 1 roughly chopped

1 (15-ounce/430-g) can cannellini beans, drained and rinsed

¼ cup (60 ml) chicken stock or water

4 slices country bread (about ½ inch/12 mm thick)

1 handful fresh parsley, roughly chopped

1 lemon, half thinly sliced, remaining half reserved

Kosher salt

1 head radicchio or treviso, halved lengthwise and thinly sliced

Flaky sea salt, for serving

In a medium saucepan, heat 2 teaspoons of the oil over medium heat. Add the sliced garlic and cook until fragrant, about 1 minute. Add the beans and stock to loosen, and cook until warmed through, 3 to 5 minutes. Using the back of a wooden spoon, smash about a quarter of the beans just enough so they hold together.

Preheat the broiler to high. Using a pastry brush, coat both sides of the bread with oil. Place it on a baking sheet and broil until the bread is golden brown, 1 to 2 minutes per side.

Roughly chop the lemon slices. Gather the parsley, lemon slices, and chopped garlic on a board and season with salt. Chop everything together until the mixture has a mostly finely chopped consistency. Transfer the mixture to a bowl, add the radicchio, and drizzle with the juice from the remaining lemon half and 1 teaspoon oil.

Divide the beans among the toasts and top with a hearty helping of the lemon-parsley relish. To finish, drizzle the crostini with oil, and sprinkle with flaky sea salt.

swoon tip

Who says plates need to match? When it comes to collecting china, buy what you love—even if that means having a handful of one-hit wonders in your cabinet. To keep your table from looking too jumbled, it's nice to include a few simple neutrals amongst the deeply colored and wildly patterned pieces.

NONNA'S CHICKEN SOUP

When I was a little peanut home sick from school, my nonna always cooked up a batch of this cold-curing chicken soup. I can still remember the aroma wafting into the living room as I reclined on the sofa watching *Gilligan's Island*. Now, when my own little peanut is sneezing, I make it for him, and—even when everyone is healthy—it's a perennial favorite. Like most soups and stews, it tastes even better the next day and freezes well, making it a super-convenient weeknight meal. The recipe isn't particularly fussy, but there are two non-negotiables: Always cook and store the pasta separately, so it doesn't turn to mush in the soup, and don't forget to pile on the pecorino—just like Nonna always did for me.

SERVES 6 TO 8

—

1 (5-pound/2.3-kg) whole chicken

1 bone-in chicken breast (about 1½ pounds/680 g)

2 yellow onions, 1 diced, 1 halved

5 or 6 carrots, peeled and cut into coins

5 stalks celery, chopped

6 cloves garlic, peeled and smashed

6 sprigs fresh thyme

3 medium parsnips, chopped

2 quarts (2 L) low-sodium chicken stock

2 teaspoons kosher salt

Freshly cracked pepper

1 pound (455 g) dried acini di pepe pasta, or another small pasta such as tubettini, orzo, or ditalini

1 small handful fresh parsley, finely chopped

Grated pecorino Romano cheese, for serving

Lemon wedges, for serving

Place the whole chicken and breast in a large stockpot. Add the onions, carrots, celery, garlic, thyme, parsnips, stock, salt, and 2 cups (480 ml) water—or enough to just cover the chicken. Season with pepper. Place the pot over medium-high heat and bring it to a simmer, skimming any foam that rises to the surface. Reduce the heat to low and gently simmer, covered, until the chicken begins to fall off the bone, about 1½ hours.

Using tongs, remove the chicken pieces, onion halves, and thyme sprigs. Discard the chicken bones and skin, then tear the meat into bite-size pieces and return it to the pot. Taste for seasoning.

Meanwhile, in a separate pot, cook the pasta according to the package directions until al dente.

To serve, place a heaping spoonful of pasta into individual bowls and ladle the soup over the pasta. Sprinkle it with parsley, pepper, and a hearty helping of cheese, and serve with lemon wedges on the side.

Leftover soup (without the pasta) can be stored in an airtight container and refrigerated for up to 3 days. The soup can also be frozen for up to 1 month.

Carrots and parsley are the only truly vibrant ingredients in this homey, ultra-comforting soup, so it's important to make them count. Cut the carrots into coins rather than the usual dice and roughly chop the parsley instead of mincing to ensure that they stand out against their neutral backdrop.

ROMAINE SALAD WITH RYE CRISPS AND LEMON-PECORINO VINAIGRETTE

This is the recipe that got my salad-phobic son to change his tune. A few years ago, we were at Roberta's—the beloved Brooklyn pizza mecca—on a Sunday afternoon and ordered a crunchy romaine salad doused in rich, lemony dressing. Convinced that he'd love it if he only gave it a try, I bribed Jivan into tasting it. (He'd been begging for a guitar.) Poor parenting, perhaps, but it worked! Now he gobbles it up every time I serve it, as does everyone else at the table. This recipe makes much more vinaigrette than you'll need, and that's not an accident. Once you taste it, you'll want a mason jar full of it in your fridge at all times. It keeps for at least a week.

SERVES 6

—

FOR THE RYE CRISPS

4 or 5 slices day-old rye bread, cut into ¼-inch (6-mm) cubes

¼ cup (60 ml) extra-virgin olive oil

2 cloves garlic, minced

A few sprigs fresh thyme or rosemary

Pinch kosher salt

FOR THE VINAIGRETTE

⅔ cup (65 g) grated pecorino-Romano cheese, plus more for serving

⅓ cup (75 ml) champagne vinegar

⅓ cup (75 ml) fresh lemon juice

1½ tablespoons Dijon mustard

1 clove garlic

2 teaspoons kosher salt

Freshly cracked pepper, plus more for serving

1½ cups (360 ml) extra-virgin olive oil

FOR THE SALAD

3 romaine hearts, ends trimmed, leaves separated, washed, and dried

1 large handful fresh mint leaves, roughly torn, some reserved for serving

Make the rye crisps: Preheat the oven to 350°F (175°C).

In a food processor, pulse the bread until coarse crumbs form. Spread the crumbs on a baking sheet and toss them with the oil, garlic, herbs, and a pinch of salt until evenly coated. Roast the crumbs, tossing occasionally, until they're golden brown, 15 to 20 minutes. Once cooled, the rye crisps can be stored in an airtight container at room temperature for up to 2 weeks.

Make the vinaigrette: In a minifood processor, pulse all of the ingredients together until they're well combined and the dressing has emulsified. (You can also whisk the dressing by hand.)

Make the salad: Place the lettuce leaves in a large bowl and scatter them with the torn mint. Pour about ¾ cup (180 ml) of the vinaigrette over the leaves, gently tossing until well coated, adding more dressing if needed. Transfer the salad to a platter and, using a fine grater, grate on additional cheese. Scatter with the rye crisps and remaining mint, and finish with freshly cracked pepper.

Flaunt the elongated elegance of romaine leaves by spreading them out on a large platter and layering on the other ingredients rather than jumbling everything together in a bowl.

KOHLRABI, APPLE, AND CELERY ROOT SALAD WITH BLACK PEPPER YOGURT

I'm always on the lookout for crisp, clean-tasting winter vegetables to serve as a counterpoint to the rich roasts and braises I cook this time of year. Kohlrabi really fits the bill. Mild and slightly sweet, it tastes almost like a broccoli stem and is delicious raw in salads. The celery root in this recipe is another cold-weather kitchen staple. To soften up its tough texture, be sure to give the sliced root a salty lemon juice bath while you prep the rest of the ingredients.

SERVES 2 TO 4

—

FOR THE SALAD

1 medium celery root (about
 12 ounces/340 g)

Pinch kosher salt

1 tablespoon extra-virgin olive oil

1½ lemons, juiced

1 medium kohlrabi

1 medium apple, such as Honeycrisp

1 small handful fresh parsley leaves,
 roughly chopped (about ½ cup/25 g),
 some reserved for serving

1 bunch watercress (about 1 cup/35 g)

3 tablespoons sunflower seeds,
 toasted and divided

Flaky sea salt, for serving

FOR THE DRESSING

1 lemon, juiced

1 teaspoon Dijon or country-style
 mustard

1 teaspoon cider vinegar

3 tablespoons extra-virgin olive oil

Salt and freshly cracked pepper

FOR THE BLACK PEPPER
YOGURT

1 cup (240 ml) full-fat plain Greek
 yogurt

20 grinds freshly cracked pepper

2 teaspoons extra-virgin olive oil

Make the salad: Trim the top and bottom of the celery root and peel off the rough skin. Cut the celery root into quarters and thinly slice it on a mandoline. Cut the slices into approximately ⅛-inch-wide (3-mm-wide) matchstick strips. Transfer the strips to a medium bowl and allow them to soften with a pinch of salt, the oil, and the juice of half a lemon.

Trim, peel, and halve the kohlrabi. Slice it into ¼-inch (6-mm) -thick half-moons and then cut it into ¼-inch-wide (6-mm-wide) matchstick strips. Transfer the strips to a bowl. Core and halve the apple and slice it into ¼-inch-thick (6-mm-thick) slices, then transfer them to the bowl with the kohlrabi. Pour the juice of 1 lemon over the kohlrabi and apple; this will prevent them from oxidizing and turning brown.

Make the dressing: In a small bowl, combine the lemon juice, mustard, and vinegar. Add the oil, whisking vigorously until the dressing is emulsified. Season with salt and pepper.

Make the black pepper yogurt: In a small bowl, mix together the yogurt, pepper, and oil, stirring until thoroughly combined.

To assemble the salad, combine the celery root with the apple and kohlrabi in a large bowl. Add the parsley, watercress, 2 tablespoons of the sunflower seeds, and the dressing. Toss until all of the ingredients are evenly coated.

To plate the salad, smear a dollop of the black pepper yogurt onto each plate and top with a helping of the salad. Sprinkle with the remaining sunflower seeds, parsley, and flaky sea salt.

The best tool for artfully smearing this yogurt—or any sauce—onto a plate is a small offset spatula, the type you'd use to frost a cake. In a pinch, the back of a spoon can also work.

BLOOD ORANGE AND ROASTED BEETS WITH YOGURT, TARRAGON, AND HAZELNUTS

Roasted beets live in my fridge all winter long. I cook up a big bunch and then use them for salads, sides, and grain bowls over the course of a week or so. This dish is a particular favorite. The blood orange not only mirrors the red and golden hues of the beets, it offsets their earthiness with a bright acidity. Here, I serve the combo on a bed of Greek yogurt, but fresh ricotta is equally delicious. If you have time, it's nice to drizzle the toasted hazelnuts with olive oil, salt, and pepper. Nuts often get shortchanged in the seasoning department!

SERVES 4
---

4 medium red beets

4 medium golden beets

2 tablespoons extra-virgin olive oil, plus extra for drizzling

Salt and freshly cracked pepper

4 or 5 sprigs fresh thyme

¼ cup (70 g) hazelnuts

3 blood oranges

1 small shallot, finely chopped

2 tablespoons red wine vinegar

¾ cup (180 ml) full-fat Greek yogurt

4 or 5 sprigs fresh tarragon

Preheat the oven to 425°F (220°C).

Place the red beets in the center of a large piece of foil. Drizzle them with oil and season with salt and pepper. Add a few thyme sprigs and tightly seal the foil around the beets to make a packet. Repeat with golden beets. Place the packets on a rimmed baking sheet and roast until the beets are tender when pierced with a knife, 45 minutes to 1 hour, depending on the size of your beets. Unwrap the beets and let them cool slightly. Remove the skin by pinching and peeling it off with your fingers, or rubbing it with a paper towel.

While the beets are roasting, toast the hazelnuts on a rimmed baking sheet for 4 to 6 minutes, or until they're golden and fragrant. Place the toasted nuts on a kitchen towel and rub them against one another to remove the skins (don't worry if all of the skins don't come off.) Roughly chop the nuts.

Squeeze the juice from half of an orange into a medium bowl. Add the shallot and vinegar. Season with salt and pepper and whisk in the oil.

Using a sharp knife, remove the pith and peel from the remaining 1½ blood oranges and slice them crosswise in ¼-inch-thick (6-mm-thick) rounds.

Cut the beets into wedges and toss them with some of the dressing, making sure to keep the golden and red beets in separate bowls.

Just before serving, season the yogurt with salt and pepper. Arrange the orange slices and beet wedges over the yogurt, spooning some of the dressing over the top. Sprinkle with the chopped hazelnuts and a healthy dose of tarragon.

For the swooniest presentation, always roast red and golden beets separately to prevent their colors from bleeding into one another.

FARRO SALAD WITH ROASTED SWEET POTATOES, RED ONION, AND GOAT CHEESE

I love me a farro salad! The hearty grain is an amazing base for all sorts of veggie combinations and it's super convenient to work with since you can cook it several days ahead. I tend to follow a loose formula: farro plus roasted veggies, a bright herb, a crunchy nut or seed, some creamy cheese, and a zingy dressing. Here, sweet potatoes and red onions caramelize gorgeously in the oven, while the earthy goat cheese and zippy vinaigrette balance out the sweetness. Feel free to play—roasted beets or winter squash would be lovely, as would hazelnuts, almonds, or feta.

SERVES 4
—

1 large sweet potato, unpeeled and sliced into ½-inch-thick (12-mm-thick) rounds, large rounds halved

1 red onion, cut into ½-inch (12-mm) wedges

4 tablespoons (60 ml) extra-virgin olive oil, divided, plus more as needed for serving

Salt and freshly cracked pepper

¾ cup (150 g) dried farro

2 tablespoons red wine vinegar

3 radishes, thinly sliced on a mandoline

1 small handful fresh dill, roughly chopped

2 tablespoons salted pistachios, roasted and roughly chopped

2 to 3 ounces (55 to 85 g) goat cheese, broken into bite-size pieces

½ lemon, juiced

Pinch smoked paprika, for serving

Flaky sea salt, for serving

Preheat the oven to 425°F (220°C).

Spread the sweet potato rounds and onion wedges on a baking sheet, drizzle with 3 tablespoons of the oil, and season with salt and pepper. Roast, shaking the baking sheet halfway through, until the sweet potatoes are golden brown and tender, 15 to 20 minutes. Let cool slightly.

Cook the farro according to the package directions. Drain.

In a medium bowl, season the warm farro with the vinegar, remaining 1 tablespoon oil, salt, and pepper. Add the sweet potato, onion, radish, dill, pistachios, and goat cheese. To finish, drizzle the salad with the lemon juice and sprinkle with smoked paprika, flaky sea salt, and pepper. If the dish seems a little dry, drizzle it with extra oil.

Neaten up the look of this delicious, disorderly dish by reserving a few precisely sliced radish rounds to sprinkle on top of the finished salad.

WINTER VEGETABLE ROAST

Peek inside my oven around six p.m. on any winter evening and you'll likely find a big tray of vegetables roasting away. This particular combination is a favorite in my family, bringing together savory caramelized root vegetables with the swoony sweetness of apples and shallots. There's no tricky technique involved here; just make sure to use enough oil and give the ingredients a little room to breathe in the pan. Overcrowded veg will never brown properly.

SERVES 6

—

2 large sweet potatoes (about 1½ pounds/680 g), quartered and cut into 1-inch (2.5-cm) wedges

2 parsnips, quartered lengthwise

1 bunch carrots (about 8 ounces/225 g), tops removed and halved lengthwise

Extra-virgin olive oil

Kosher salt and freshly cracked pepper

4 sprigs fresh rosemary, divided

20 sprigs fresh thyme, divided, plus more for serving

6 large shallots, peeled and quartered

3 medium McIntosh apples, cored and sliced into 1-inch (2.5-cm) wedges

Flaky sea salt, for serving

Preheat the oven to 400°F (205°C).

Arrange the sweet potato wedges, parsnips, and carrots on a large baking sheet and drizzle them generously with oil. Season with salt and pepper and half of the herbs and toss until the vegetables are evenly coated. Place the shallots and apples on a separate baking sheet and drizzle them generously with oil. Season with salt and pepper and the remaining herbs and toss to coat.

Roast the vegetables for 15 minutes, then remove the baking sheet from the oven and shake to redistribute the vegetables. Return it to the oven along with the apples and shallots, and roast until everything is golden brown and tender, 25 to 30 minutes. (The apples often need a little extra time to brown.) Remove both sheets from the oven and set them aside to cool slightly before tossing everything together in a large bowl. Before serving, finish with flaky sea salt and a sprinkling of thyme leaves.

If carrots are sliced thinly enough—vertically in half for slim roots or in quarters for thicker ones—they'll curl up alluringly when roasted. Serve them on a plain, pale platter to really show off their shape.

PAN-SEARED TANGY BRUSSELS SPROUTS

A limp sprout is a big bummer, as far as I'm concerned. But it's easy to avoid that sorry fate if you know this secret: It's all about dry, room-temperature sprouts and a big, hot pan. If the temperature of the pan is too low, the sprouts too cold or damp, or the skillet too crowded, the little suckers will never get really crispy. This recipe lays it all out for you. Follow it precisely, and you'll end up with a stellar winter side dish—crunchy, smoky, sweet, tangy, and delicious.

SERVES 2 TO 4

—

¼ cup (60 ml) extra-virgin olive oil plus more as needed for drizzling

1½ pounds (680 g) Brussels sprouts, trimmed and halved, loose leaves reserved

1 shallot, thinly sliced

1 tablespoon finely chopped fresh rosemary

¼ teaspoon finely diced red Fresno chile, plus a few thin rounds for serving

2 tablespoons honey

2 tablespoons white wine vinegar

Salt and freshly cracked black pepper

1 lemon, zested

Flaky sea salt, for serving

In a large cast-iron skillet, heat the oil over medium-high heat. Add the Brussels sprouts and loose leaves and cook, stirring only occasionally, until golden and crisp on all sides, 8 to 10 minutes. Add the shallots, rosemary, and chile, and cook until the shallots are soft and translucent, 2 to 3 minutes; if the pan dries out in the process, add a good drizzle of oil. Add the honey and vinegar and toss until the sprouts and leaves are evenly coated. Continue to cook until the mixture is heated through and the pan is deglazed, 1 to 2 minutes. Taste and season with salt and pepper. Transfer the sprouts to a bowl and garnish with the lemon zest, a few thinly sliced chile rounds, and flaky sea salt.

swoon tip

Tiny but mighty, one red chile pepper plays two key roles in this dish, adding both a zip of spice and a flash of contrasting color. To maximize the pepper's potential, cut it in two ways: a fine dice to deliver evenly dispersed heat and thin slices for a bright visual pop.

ROASTED SUNCHOKES WITH ORANGE, MARCONA ALMONDS, AND PECORINO TOSCANO

My first experience with sunchokes coincided with my inaugural visit to Franny's, the Brooklyn restaurant that almost single-handedly shifted the way I think about food. Our waiter suggested I order the sunchoke starter, and I admit I was utterly confused when the knobby little nuggets, which look like something out of Hogwarts, were set down in front of me. But once I tasted them, I was hooked! Sweet and nutty with a creamy interior, they're fantastic paired with bright and sharp flavors like the Cara Cara oranges, pickled shallots, and pecorino Toscano in this recipe. The little roots, also known as Jerusalem artichokes, do vary greatly in size and shape. Make sure to cut them into relatively equal pieces so they roast at the same rate.

SERVES 4

—

2 pounds (910 g) sunchokes, rinsed, dried, and quartered

Extra-virgin olive oil, for drizzling

Salt

¼ cup (25 grams) Pickled Shallots (page 268)

1 Cara Cara orange, zested and supremed

¼ cup (35 g) salted Marcona almonds

Pecorino Toscano cheese, for shaving

Flaky sea salt and freshly cracked pepper, for serving

Preheat the oven to 425°F (220°C). Spread the sunchokes on a baking sheet and drizzle them very generously with oil. Season with salt and toss until evenly coated. Roast the sunchokes, tossing them halfway through, until they're deep golden and crispy, about 40 minutes.

Allow the sunchokes to cool slightly, then toss them with the shallot, orange segments, and almonds. Sprinkle the sunchokes with the orange zest and shaved cheese. Season with flaky sea salt and freshly cracked pepper.

Don't cast aside a well-loved bowl or platter just because it has a chip or two. Little imperfections add soul to the table, and are especially suited to serving up homey recipes like this one.

MEZZI RIGATONI
WITH RADICCHIO AND GUANCIALE

If you've never tried the perfectly crispy little nuggets of goodness known as guanciale, you need to, stat! Made from pig cheeks, the cured meat is often compared to pancetta—though I'd contend that this little piggy is in a league of its own. Guanciale has a sweeter, less salty flavor, and its texture, especially when cubed and sautéed, is truly melt-in-your-mouth. In this recipe, bitter radicchio cuts through that delicious richness, and bread crumbs add a lovely crunch. You could also try it with Brussels sprouts or bitter greens, and—in a pinch—pancetta, but it's worth going the extra mile to get your hands on some genuine sweet cheeks.

SERVES 4

—

¾ to 1 pound (340 to 455 g) dried mezzi rigatoni

1 tablespoon extra-virgin olive oil, plus more for drizzling

6 ounces (170 g) guanciale or pancetta, cut into ¼-inch (6-mm) cubes

6 cloves garlic, chopped

½ teaspoon Aleppo pepper, plus more for serving

1 head radicchio, quartered, cored, and cut into ½-inch (12-mm) strips

½ cup (50 g) grated pecorino Romano cheese, plus more for serving

2 lemons, 1 zested, both juiced

Salt and freshly cracked pepper

Toasted Bread Crumbs (page 269), for serving

1 small handful fresh parsley, roughly chopped for serving

Bring a large pot of salted water to a rapid boil over medium-high heat. Add the rigatoni and cook according to the package directions, until al dente. Reserve 1 cup (240 ml) of the cooking water, then drain the pasta.

While the pasta is cooking, heat the oil in a large skillet over medium heat. Add the guanciale and cook until golden brown and crisp on all sides, 4 to 5 minutes. Using a slotted spoon, transfer the guanciale to a paper towel–lined plate.

Pour off all but 3 to 4 tablespoons of fat from the skillet. Add the garlic and Aleppo pepper and cook until the garlic is light golden, about 1 minute. Add the radicchio and cook just until it begins to wilt, about 2 minutes.

Toss the pasta and cheese together with the radicchio mixture in the skillet over very low heat. Add the reserved cooking water, ¼ cup (60 ml) at a time, as needed, to make a light sauce. Stir in the lemon juice and guanciale and drizzle with a bit of oil to finish. Check your seasoning. Transfer the pasta to a bowl and garnish with the bread crumbs, lemon zest, parsley, pecorino, Aleppo pepper, and a few grinds of freshly cracked black pepper.

The majestic magenta hue of radicchio fades quickly when exposed to heat, turning a murky brown. To avoid that fate, err on the side of undercooking it, allowing the warm pasta to finish the wilting process once the dish is tossed together in the pan.

PACCHERI WITH PORK SHOULDER RAGU AND CREAMY GOAT CHEESE

Al di la was one of the first Brooklyn restaurants I fell in love with; Victor and I were regulars long before Jivan was born. My all-time favorite al di la dish is actually a special: paccheri with braised pork ragu. Once Jivan started joining us for dinners out, he, too, became obsessed with this meaty sauce, and I became obsessed with trying to re-create it for him at home. After at least twenty-five failed attempts, I finally decided to just ask Chef Anna Klinger for the recipe. The result was everything I'd been craving—rich and meaty, with notes of sage and fennel. I've changed up the ingredients and method very slightly here, but this recipe is heavily inspired by Anna's—and I can't thank her enough.

SERVES 6 TO 8

—

4 pounds (1.8 kg) boneless pork shoulder, excess fat trimmed, cut into 2-inch (5-cm) pieces

Salt and freshly cracked pepper

2 tablespoons extra-virgin olive oil

2 sprigs fresh rosemary

3 sprigs fresh sage

1 cup (240 ml) dry white wine

5 cups (1.2 L) low-sodium chicken stock (enough to just cover the meat)

4 tablespoons (2 ounces/55 g) unsalted butter

2 teaspoons fennel seeds, toasted and lightly crushed

2 carrots, finely chopped

1 stalk celery, finely chopped

1 onion, finely chopped

4 cloves garlic, chopped

1 teaspoon red pepper flakes

1 cup (240 ml) whole milk

1 (28-ounce/785-g) can crushed San Marzano tomatoes

1 tablespoon tomato paste

1 pound (455 g) dried paccheri or rigatoni

4 ounces (115 g) goat cheese

½ cup (50 g) coarsely grated pecorino Romano cheese

4 sprigs fresh parsley, chopped

Freshly cracked pepper, for serving

Preheat the oven to 325°F (165°C).

Season the pork generously with salt and pepper. In a large Dutch oven, heat the oil over medium-high heat. Working in two batches, sear half the pork until well browned on all sides, about 12 minutes per batch. Using a slotted spoon, transfer the pork to a large plate, then repeat with the remaining meat. Drain all but 2 tablespoons of the fat from the pot. Tie the rosemary and sage into a bundle with kitchen twine, then add it to the pot along with the wine. Using a wooden spoon, scrape up any browned bits of pork stuck to the bottom of the pot. Simmer over medium-low heat until the wine has reduced by half. Return the pork to the pot, pour in the stock, and bring it to a simmer. Cover the pot with a tight-fitting lid and place it in the oven. Cook for 1½ to 2 hours, or until the pork is very tender.

Using a slotted spoon, transfer the pork to a platter. Skim the fat off the top of the braising liquid and return the pot to the stove. Bring the braising liquid to a boil and boil vigorously for approximately 30 minutes, until the liquid has reduced to about 1 cup (240 ml). Meanwhile, shred the pork with a fork.

Transfer the reduced braising liquid to a small bowl. Return the pot to the stove and melt the butter over medium heat. Add the fennel seeds, carrots, celery, onion, and garlic and sauté until the onion is soft and translucent, 6 to 8 minutes. Stir in the red pepper flakes and sauté for 1 minute. Add the milk, tomatoes, tomato paste, pork, and reserved braising liquid. Simmer, uncovered, until the flavors meld and the ragu thickens slightly, 45 minutes to 1 hour. Taste for seasoning.

Meanwhile, bring a large pot of salted water to a rapid boil over medium-high heat. Add the paccheri and cook according to the package directions, until al dente. Drain the pasta.

In a small bowl, combine the goat cheese and ⅓ cup (75 ml) warm water, stirring vigorously until it takes on a smooth, creamy consistency, similar to sour cream.

To serve, divide the pasta among bowls and pile each serving with the ragu. Top with some grated cheese, chopped parsley, and a dollop of goat cheese, and season with freshly cracked pepper.

Ragu is rustic by nature, but I like to give it a slightly more elegant edge when entertaining by plating individual portions, topping each serving with coarsely grated pecorino, a bit of goat cheese, and a sprinkling of bright green parsley. Be sure to thin out the goat cheese with enough water; you want soft dollops, not graceless blobs.

SLOW-ROASTED COD WITH GRAPEFRUIT, CAPER, AND JALAPEÑO RELISH

While I love a seared, crispy-skinned piece of fish, it's not really a party-friendly preparation. Who wants to stand at the stove fussing over fillets with a house full of hungry guests? Instead, when serving a crowd, I pop my fish into the oven and slow roast it, serving it up with a bright relish that I've made in advance. The result: Everyone thinks I have it all together. (Smoke and mirrors, people, smoke and mirrors!) The relish is quite forgiving when it comes to substitutions: Feel free to use thinly sliced red onion instead of green onions and orange or lemon instead of grapefruit. One thing to note is that citrus releases quite a bit of liquid over time. If you make the relish in advance and it gets watery, just drain it a touch and add a little olive oil before serving.

SERVES 4
—

¼ cup plus 1 tablespoon (75 ml) extra-virgin olive oil, divided

2 pounds (910 g) cod fillets

7 green onions, trimmed, divided

Salt and freshly cracked pepper

2 medium pink grapefruits

1 jalapeño, seeded and finely chopped

2 tablespoons capers

¼ cup (13 g) lightly packed fresh mint leaves, torn if large

1 lime, zested and juiced

Preheat the oven to 275°F (135°C). Pour ¼ cup (60 ml) of the oil into a medium skillet or shallow baking dish. Add the fish and 4 green onions and turn the fish until evenly coated in oil. Season with salt and pepper. Roast until the fish is just opaque throughout, 15 to 25 minutes, depending on its thickness.

While the fish roasts, remove the pith and peel from the grapefruits. Working over a bowl, segment the flesh, reserving any juices. Thinly slice the remaining green onions. Add them to the bowl with the jalapeño, capers, and remaining 1 tablespoon oil. Stir to combine and season with salt and pepper. Just before serving, stir in the mint.

Sprinkle the fish with the lime zest and drizzle it with the lime juice. Top with spoonfuls of the grapefruit relish and serve alongside the roasted green onions.

Supreming a pink grapefruit shows off its rosy flesh to best advantage—and the technique isn't difficult once you get the hang of it. First, slice off the top and bottom of the fruit, then run a knife (a thin, flexible serrated one works best) along the sides to remove the peel and pith. Finally, working over a bowl, cut along each natural seam, just inside the membranes, allowing the succulent little segments to drop into the bowl as you slice.

SALT-ENCRUSTED RED SNAPPER WITH WINTER CITRUS AND SALSA VERDE

Salt-baked fish always takes me back to the tiny Spanish island of Formentera, where I first tasted it at a seaside cafe more than fifteen years ago. It's a true showstopper, with a pristine white crust burnished ever so slightly by the heat. And while it looks like special occasion food—I always make it for Christmas Day—it's actually simple to prepare. If, judging by the name, you're expecting a total salt bomb, fear not. The salt simply serves as a shell, trapping in both the natural moisture of the fish and the aromatic juices of the herbs and citrus. Try it once and, like me, you'll be addicted.

SERVES 4

—

1 (4 to 5 pounds/1.8 to 2.3 kg total) whole red snapper, cleaned

5 egg whites

3 pounds (1.4 kg) kosher salt

2 oranges, sliced into rounds

3 lemons, sliced into rounds

1 small bunch fresh rosemary or chives

1 small bunch fresh tarragon

1 small bunch fresh thyme

Salt and freshly cracked pepper

Extra-virgin olive oil, for drizzling

1 shallot, thinly sliced into rounds

3 cloves garlic, smashed

Lemon wedges for serving

Salsa Verde (page 266), for serving

Preheat the oven to 450°F (230°C). Rinse the fish under cold water and pat it dry.

Place the egg whites in a large bowl. Using a hand-held electric mixer or whisk, beat the egg whites until soft peaks form, then fold in the salt until the mixture resembles wet sand. If the mixture is too dry, add water, 1 tablespoon at a time.

Spread a thin layer of the salt mixture on a baking sheet that's just large enough to hold the fish. Top the salt with a third of the citrus slices, then scatter with a third of the herbs. Place the fish on top. Season the cavity of the fish with salt and pepper, and drizzle with oil. Stuff the fish with another third of the citrus slices and herbs, as well as the shallot and garlic. Lightly drizzle the outside of the fish with oil. Place the remaining citrus slices and herbs on top of the fish, then cover with the remaining salt mixture until the fish is totally encased (it's okay if the tail peeks out).

Bake for 35 minutes. Remove the fish from the oven and let it sit for 10 minutes. Using a heavy knife or spoon, crack the salt shell and brush the salt from the fish. Carefully remove and discard the skin, then fillet the meat; it should lift easily from the bones.

Serve the fish with the salsa verde and lemon wedges on the side.

Never squander an opportunity for drama! Make sure your guests have a chance to ooh and aaah over the whole snapper in all its glory before you fillet the fish.

PAN-SEARED BASS OVER BLACK LENTILS WITH PARSLEY-LIME SAUCE

I crave fresh, vibrant flavors all year long—not just in summer. But during chillier months, I like to cozy up that brightness with something homier. This fish dish, with warmly spiced black lentils and herbal, zippy lime salsa verde, is a prime example. The lentils are a staple in my house; I toss them into salads and even eat them for breakfast, topped with a poached egg. As with all beans and legumes, I like to add a touch of vinegar and a little hint of cumin to complement their earthy flavor. They store well in the fridge for up to five days, so consider cooking a big ol' batch.

SERVES 4

—

FOR THE LENTILS AND FISH

3 tablespoons extra-virgin olive oil, divided

2 medium shallots, finely diced

2 small cloves garlic, finely diced

1 stalk celery, finely diced

1 small carrot, finely diced

1 fennel bulb, half finely diced, half shaved on a mandoline

1½ teaspoons ground cumin

2 cups (480 ml) low-sodium chicken stock

1 teaspoon white wine vinegar

1 cup (190 g) black lentils

Salt and freshly cracked pepper

4 striped bass fillets, about 6 ounces (170 g) each (if possible, get the center cut)

FOR THE PARSLEY-LIME SAUCE

½ cup (25 g) lightly packed fresh parsley

¼ cup (10 g) lightly packed fresh cilantro

1 small handful fresh chives, chopped (about 3 tablespoons)

1 clove garlic, chopped

½ cup (120 ml) extra-virgin olive oil, plus more if desired

1 lime, zested

2½ tablespoons fresh lime juice, plus more if desired

½ serrano chile, seeded and minced

Make the lentils: In a medium saucepan, heat 2 tablespoons of the oil over medium heat. Add the shallots and garlic and cook until soft and translucent, 2 to 3 minutes. Add the celery, carrot, and diced fennel. Sauté, stirring occasionally, until the vegetables are just beginning to soften, 2 to 3 minutes. Add the cumin and cook until fragrant, 1 minute. Add the stock, vinegar, and lentils. Bring to a boil, then reduce the heat to a simmer. Partially cover and gently simmer until the lentils are tender but retain their shape, 20 to 25 minutes. Season to taste with salt and pepper.

Make the parsley-lime sauce: In the bowl of a food processor, pulse together the parsley, cilantro, chives, and garlic. Slowly pour in the oil and process until the leaves are very finely chopped and a loose sauce has formed. Transfer it to a small mixing bowl and stir in the lime zest, juice, and chile. Season to taste with salt and pepper. Feel free to adjust the flavors and texture to your personal preference, adding extra lime juice or olive oil if desired.

Pat the fish dry with a paper towel and season both sides with salt and pepper.

Make the fish: In a large, heavy-bottomed skillet, heat the remaining 1 tablespoon oil over medium-high heat. Place the fillets skin-side down and sear until golden and crispy, 3 to 4 minutes. Flip the fillets over and cook until just opaque throughout, 2 to 3 minutes more, depending on their thickness.

To serve, place the fish on a bed of warm lentils. Drizzle the parsley-lime sauce around the lentils and over the fish. Garnish with the shaved fennel.

To produce gorgeously feathery slices of fennel, start by dividing the bulb in quarters and paring away most, but not all, of the core. Next, carefully shave each quarter lengthwise on your mandoline. Make sure to slice the fennel paper thin to combat the veg's natural toughness.

BRAISED SHORT RIBS WITH HORSERADISH BREAD CRUMBS AND CELERIAC PUREE

Red wine–braised short ribs are a Calderone classic, both for snow days and holidays. Because the meat is so rich and silky, it benefits from a spicy-zesty-crunchy gremolata to brighten it up and add some texture. And in place of traditional mash, I spike my pureed potatoes with celery root, which has a slightly sweet, nutty, and refreshing taste.

SERVES 6
—

FOR THE SHORT RIBS

5 pounds (2.3 kg) bone-in beef short ribs, cut into 6 to 8 pieces

Kosher salt and freshly cracked pepper

¼ cup (60 ml) olive oil

4 ounces (115 g) pancetta, chopped

1 tablespoon fennel seeds, toasted and crushed

1 medium onion, finely chopped

5 cloves garlic, smashed

1 leek, halved and chopped

6 sprigs fresh thyme

4 carrots, peeled and cut into 1-inch (2.5-cm) chunks on the bias

2 stalks celery, cut into 1-inch (2.5-cm) pieces

1 (750-ml) bottle full-bodied red wine

2 tablespoons tomato paste

2 tablespoons red wine vinegar

2 to 3 cups (480 to 720 ml) beef stock

FOR THE CELERIAC PUREE

2 cups (480 ml) whole milk

2 tablespoons kosher salt

1½ pounds (680 g) celeriac, peeled and cut into 1½-inch (4-cm) pieces

1½ pounds (680 g) Yukon Gold potatoes, peeled and cut into 1½-inch (4-cm) pieces

1 leek, white and pale green parts only, halved

½ stick (2 ounces/55 g) unsalted butter, softened

Salt and freshly ground white pepper

Horseradish Bread Crumbs (page 271), for serving

Preheat the oven to 350°F (175°C).

Make the short ribs: Season the short ribs with salt and pepper. In a large Dutch oven, heat the oil over medium-high heat. Working in batches, sear the short ribs until well browned on all sides, about 10 minutes. Using a slotted spoon, transfer the short ribs to a large plate.

Drain all but 1 to 2 tablespoons of fat from the pot and add the pancetta. Cook, stirring occasionally, until it begins to brown, 5 to 7 minutes. Add the crushed fennel seeds, onion, garlic, leek, thyme, carrots, and celery. Cook, stirring occasionally, for 5 to 7 minutes, or until the leeks have softened. Add the wine, tomato paste, vinegar, and stock and bring them to a boil. Return the short ribs to the pot, adding extra stock just to cover if necessary. Cover the pot and put it in the oven.

Cook for 2½ hours. Remove the pot from the oven and transfer the short ribs and carrots to a large platter; discard the thyme. Strain the cooking liquid through a fine-mesh sieve into a bowl, then return the strained liquid to the pot. Bring it to a boil, then reduce the heat to medium and simmer for 20 to 25 minutes, or until the liquid has reduced by half. Skim any excess fat on the surface. Return the short ribs to the pot, turning them so they're evenly coated, and season with salt and pepper.

Make the celeriac puree: In a medium saucepan, combine the milk, salt, celeriac, potatoes, leek, and 2 cups (480 ml) water and simmer, covered, until the celeriac and potatoes are tender, 20 to 25 minutes. Drain the potatoes, reserving 1 cup (240 ml) of the liquid. Transfer the celeriac, potatoes, and leek to a food processor and puree them with the butter until they're smooth, creamy, and free of lumps. If the puree is too thick, add some of the reserved cooking liquid. Season with salt and pepper.

Divide the celeriac puree among individual plates. Top with the short ribs, carrots, and sauce and serve accompanied by the horseradish bread crumbs.

Even an ultra-rustic braise deserves one fancy touch. Here, the carrots are sliced on the bias to play up their lanky, elegant shape. It might sound like a minor detail, but a simple nod to aesthetics often goes a long way.

SUNDAY LAMB ROAST WITH FENNEL, ROOT VEGETABLES, AND LEMON CHERMOULA

Rack of lamb is a classic special occasion meal—there's something inherently festive about an abundant row of neat little chops. This version gets an exotic touch from Moroccan chermoula, a mélange of dried spices and fresh herbs that doubles as a marinade and a finishing sauce. (If you haven't noticed by now, in my kitchen, lamb and Moroccan flavors go together like peanut butter and jelly.) While it looks—and tastes—quite fancy, this dish is actually quite simple to pull off. The lamb is simply seared and then finished in the oven on a bed of caramelized fennel and beets, which soak up all of its deliciously savory juices.

SERVES 4 TO 6
—

FOR THE CHERMOULA

2 cups (80 g) lightly packed fresh cilantro

2 cups (100 g) lightly packed fresh parsley

4 cloves garlic, chopped

1 tablespoon cumin seeds, lightly toasted

2 teaspoons coriander seeds, lightly toasted

2 teaspoons hot paprika

¼ teaspoon cayenne pepper

⅓ cup (75 ml) extra-virgin olive oil

2 lemons, zested and juiced

½ teaspoon kosher salt

Freshly cracked pepper

FOR THE LAMB

4 medium beets, peeled and cut into 1-inch (2.5-cm) wedges

2 fennel bulbs, quartered, cored, and cut into 2-inch (5-cm) wedges, fronds reserved

Extra-virgin olive oil, for drizzling

Salt and freshly cracked pepper

2 racks of lamb (about 1½ pounds/680 g each)

2 teaspoons canola oil

1 lemon, juiced

Make the chermoula: Place the cilantro, parsley, and garlic in the bowl of a food processor. Pulse to roughly chop. Add the spices and olive oil and process until a paste forms. Add the zest from 1 lemon (reserving the remainder for serving) and 2 tablespoons of the juice to the food processor, pulsing until combined. Add the salt and season with pepper. Divide the chermoula evenly between two bowls. Combine the remaining lemon juice with one bowl of chermoula; you'll use this for serving. Reserve the less lemony chermoula for coating the lamb.

Make the lamb: Preheat the oven to 425°F (220°C). Spread the beets and fennel bulbs on a baking sheet, drizzle them generously with olive oil, and season with salt and pepper. Toss until the vegetables are evenly coated. Roast until the vegetables are browned on one side, 20 to 25 minutes.

While the vegetables are roasting, pat the lamb dry and season it generously with salt and pepper. In a large cast-iron or other heavy-bottomed skillet, heat the canola oil over medium-high heat. Add the lamb fatty-side down, in batches if necessary, and sear on all sides until well browned, 12 to 15 minutes total. Transfer the lamb to a baking sheet and rub the racks on all sides with the less lemony chermoula.

Reduce the oven to 400°F (205°C). Stir the vegetables and place the racks of lamb directly on top of them. Roast until the vegetables are tender and caramelized and the lamb registers 125°F to 135°F (51°C to 57°C) on an instant-read thermometer for medium-rare, about 20 minutes.

Sprinkle the lamb and vegetables with the reserved lemon zest and drizzle with the juice of the remaining lemon. Garnish with the reserved fennel fronds and serve with the reserved chermoula on the side.

For the sake of both flavor and appearance, roasted food always benefits from a bright, fresh topping. Here, lacy fennel fronds and vibrant lemon zest liven up the look and taste of the rich, earthy dish.

WHOLE ROASTED CHICKEN WITH SUMAC, ROASTED VEGETABLES, AND SESAME LABNE

Even after I found my confidence in the kitchen, the idea of roasting a whole chicken continued to intimidate me for years. Finally, one night, bored with my usual family dinner rotation, I decided to try it—and I couldn't believe how easy it was! With almost no prep time, you get a delicious, no-fail, one-pan dinner that's quick enough for Wednesday and impressive enough for Saturday night. This version gets its Middle Eastern flavor profile from one of my new favorite spices: sumac. The ground berry's rusty hue might lead you to think it has a peppery taste, but in fact it boasts a tangy, lemon-like flavor that's incredibly versatile. The labne—an ultra-thick, creamy yogurt—is another delicious Mediterranean touch. If you can't find it, Greek yogurt is a fine substitute.

SERVES 2 TO 3
—

1 (4-pound/1.8 kg) chicken

2 tablespoons unsalted butter, cut into small pieces and softened

2 teaspoons kosher salt, plus extra for seasoning

3 teaspoons sumac, divided, plus more for serving

3 lemons, halved

3 heads garlic, halved

4 carrots, peeled and quartered

4 small Yukon Gold potatoes, scrubbed and quartered (about 1½ pounds/680 g)

2 small yellow onions, quartered

½ cup (120 ml) extra-virgin olive oil, plus more for drizzling

Freshly cracked pepper

1 cup (240 ml) labne or full-fat Greek yogurt

Toasted sesame seeds, for serving

Flaky sea salt, for serving

Place the chicken in a large roasting pan. Using your fingers, gently separate the skin from the flesh across the breasts and drumsticks. Rub the butter between the skin and the flesh. Rub the salt and 2 teaspoons of the sumac all over the chicken. If time permits, refrigerate the chicken, uncovered, for at least 6 hours and up to overnight.

Preheat the oven to 425°F (220°C). Squeeze half of one lemon over the chicken and place it inside the cavity along with a half head of garlic. Scatter the carrots, potatoes, onions, and remaining lemons and garlic around the chicken. Drizzle the vegetables and chicken with the ½ cup (120 ml) oil. Sprinkle the vegetables with the remaining 1 teaspoon sumac and season with salt and pepper, tossing until the vegetables are evenly coated. Roast, tossing the vegetables occasionally, until the chicken and vegetables are deep golden and cooked through and the chicken registers 165°F (72°C) in the thickest part of the thigh, about 1 hour and 15 minutes. Allow the chicken to rest for 10 minutes before carving.

Drizzle the labne with oil and sprinkle it with the sesame seeds, some pepper, sumac, and flaky sea salt. Serve it alongside the chicken.

Roasting a gorgeously golden chicken isn't difficult, but it does help to think ahead. Chilling the bird, uncovered, for at least six hours dries out its surface, allowing the skin to caramelize and crisp up beautifully in the oven.

EARL GREY CHOCOLATE SOUFFLÉ CAKE WITH CANDIED KUMQUATS

I first made this cake ten years ago, for Jivan's nursery school potluck dinner. The other parents lost their minds over the slightly gooey confection, which is both rich and lighter than air. It quickly became my claim to fame, and I was asked to make it again the next year. The third year, I decided to get a little fancy and bring one of those instant whipped cream makers. I was so proud of my new toy that I gathered the other parents to show them how it worked. And you can probably guess where this is going . . . I pulled the trigger and whipped cream exploded onto every guest, the ceiling, the artwork-covered walls. But, lo and behold, the other parents did request the cake again for the next potluck—it's that good! And now I always hand-whip my cream, like an honest baker should.

SERVES 8 TO 10

—

FOR THE CAKE

1 stick (4 ounces/115 g) unsalted butter, cut into 8 pieces, plus extra for the pan

⅓ cup (75 ml) milk

4 Earl Grey tea bags

12 ounces (340 g) fine-quality bittersweet chocolate, chopped

½ teaspoon pure vanilla extract

¼ teaspoon kosher salt

⅔ cup (135 g) sugar, divided

5 large eggs, separated and at room temperature

1 tablespoon all-purpose flour

Cocoa powder, for dusting the cake

Lightly sweetened fresh whipped cream, for serving

FOR THE CANDIED KUMQUATS

½ cup (100 g) sugar

20 kumquats, cut crosswise into thin slices (2 cups/450 g)

Make the cake: Preheat the oven to 350°F (175°C). Grease a 9-inch (23-cm) springform pan with butter, fit the bottom with a round of parchment paper, and grease the paper.

In a small saucepan, heat the milk over medium-high heat until simmering. Remove it from the heat and put the tea bags in the milk to steep. Cover for 10 minutes, then remove the tea bags, squeezing out any excess liquid. Set aside.

Combine the chocolate and butter in a large metal bowl, set it over a saucepan of simmering water, and stir frequently until the chocolate and butter are completely melted. Remove from the heat and let the mixture cool completely. Whisk in the infused milk, vanilla extract, salt, and ⅓ cup (65 g) of the sugar. Add the egg yolks one at a time, whisking well after each addition. Whisk in the flour.

In a medium bowl, use an electric mixer set at medium-high speed to beat the egg whites together with a pinch of salt. Beat until soft peaks form, then add the remaining ⅓ cup (65 g) sugar a little at a time, and continue beating the whites until they hold stiff, glossy peaks.

Whisk about a quarter of the egg whites into the chocolate mixture, then use a rubber spatula to gently fold in the remainder. Pour the batter into the springform pan, spreading it evenly across the pan. Bake for 28 to 30 minutes, or until the cake's center is slightly gooey and its edges pull away from the pan.

Make the candied kumquats: In a small saucepan, bring 1 cup (240 ml) water and the sugar to boil over medium-high heat until the sugar has dissolved. Add the kumquat slices, then reduce the heat to medium and simmer, stirring occasionally, until the kumquats are tender and translucent, about 15 minutes.

When the cake is finished baking, transfer it to a wire rack and let it cool for 10 minutes, then gently unmold it from the pan and let it cool to room temperature. Dust the top with cocoa powder.

Serve each piece of cake piled with the whipped cream and a spoonful of candied kumquats.

swoon tip

Don't attempt to tidy up this beautifully imperfect confection. Cracks in the surface and crumbs on the plate only add to the appeal of a fallen soufflé. Rather than whitewashing them with confectioners' sugar, add to the mess by finishing with a dusting of cocoa.

BLOOD ORANGE BUNDT CAKE
WITH ORANGE BITTERS GLAZE

How do you know you're a truly obsessive baker? When you sip a delicious new cocktail and your first thought is, "These flavors would be even better in a cake!" That's what happened when I discovered the explosively tasty combination of bourbon, blood orange, and bitters recently—and the result is this perfectly moist and fluffy Bundt. Developing the recipe took some trial and error: On my first attempt, I burned the cake. And then I had to experiment with the flour to fat ratio to get just the right texture. But try, try again paid off: This spiked sweet is sophisticated, indulgent, and a seriously winning winter dinner party dessert.

SERVES 8 TO 10
—

FOR THE CAKE

Butter, for greasing the pan

3 or 4 blood oranges

¼ cup (60 ml) fresh lemon juice

2 cups (250 g) all-purpose flour, plus extra for the pan

½ cup (60 g) almond meal

1½ teaspoons baking powder

½ teaspoon baking soda

1½ teaspoons kosher salt

5 large eggs

2 cups (400 g) granulated sugar

¾ cup (180 ml) extra-virgin olive oil

½ cup (120 ml) full-fat plain Greek yogurt

2 tablespoons bourbon

FOR THE GLAZE

1½ cups (190 g) confectioners' sugar

3 teaspoons fresh blood orange juice

2 teaspoons fresh lemon juice

1 tablespoon bourbon

6 drops orange bitters

1 teaspoon blood orange zest

Make the cake: Position a rack in the middle of the oven and preheat the oven to 350°F (175°C). Generously grease a 12-cup (2.8-L) Bundt pan with butter and dust it with flour, tapping out the excess. Set aside.

Using a Microplane, grate the zest of 3 of the oranges. Squeeze ½ cup (120 ml) juice, using the fourth orange if necessary. Combine the orange juice with the lemon juice.

In a small bowl, whisk together the flour, almond meal, baking powder, baking soda, and salt until just combined.

In the bowl of a stand mixer fitted with the paddle attachment, beat the eggs on medium-high speed until they're frothy and evenly colored. Slowly add the granulated sugar, beating until the mixture is thick and fluffy, about 3 minutes. Reduce the mixer speed to low and alternately add the flour mixture and oil, beginning and ending with the flour mixture and mixing just until each addition is incorporated. Scrape down the sides of the bowl if necessary. With the mixer still on low speed, add the yogurt, bourbon, orange and lemon juices, and orange zest, mixing just until everything is incorporated.

Pour the batter into the prepared pan, leaving about 1 inch (2.5 cm) between the batter and the top of the pan. Bake the cake for 35 to 40 minutes, or until a knife or cake tester inserted into the center comes out with a few crumbs still clinging to it. Transfer the cake to a wire rack and allow it to cool in the pan for 15 minutes before unmolding and cooling it completely on the rack.

Make the glaze: Over a medium bowl, sift the confectioners' sugar through a sieve to remove any lumps. Whisk in the orange and lemon juices, bourbon, and bitters. Stir in the zest. If the glaze is too runny, you can add more sugar; if it's too thick, add more juice.

When the cake has cooled completely and is still sitting on the rack, drizzle it generously with the glaze and then transfer it to a serving platter.

---

swoon tip

An intricately detailed pan makes for a gorgeous cake, but all of those little nooks and crannies do increase the risk of sticking. A good rule of thumb: The more decorative the pan, the more you need to grease it. Butter is a Bundt's best friend!

BUTTERSCOTCH POTS DE CRÈME WITH SALTED CARAMEL TAHINI SAUCE AND TOASTED KASHA

I first encountered butterscotch pots de crème at Gjelina—the super-swoony restaurant in Venice, California—and then re-created them for Christmas a few years ago, adding my own twist with toasted kasha and salted caramel tahini sauce. Because oven temps and ramekins vary, you have to keep an eye on these little custards. You'll know they're ready when they're thick but still wobble in the center. They'll firm up further in the fridge.

MAKES 6 SERVINGS

—

FOR THE POTS DE CRÈME

2 cups (480 ml) heavy cream

1 cup (240 ml) whole milk

1 vanilla bean, halved lengthwise and scraped

½ stick (2 ounces/55 g) unsalted butter

¾ cup (165 g) packed light brown sugar

½ teaspoon kosher salt

6 large egg yolks, at room temperature

Flaky sea salt, for serving

Unsweetened fresh whipped cream, for serving

1 tablespoon black sesame seeds, toasted, for serving

1 recipe Toasted Kasha (page 271), for serving

FOR THE CARAMEL SAUCE

¾ cup (150 g) granulated sugar

½ cup (120 ml) heavy cream

2 tablespoons unsalted butter

¾ teaspoon kosher salt

2 tablespoons tahini

½ teaspoon fresh lemon juice

Make the pots de crème: Position a rack in the middle of the oven and preheat the oven to 300°F (150°C). Put six (6-ounce/180-ml) ramekins into a baking pan.

Bring the cream and milk to a boil over medium heat in a small saucepan and then remove from heat. Add the vanilla bean seeds and pod, cover, and infuse while you prepare the custard.

In a medium saucepan, melt the butter over medium heat. Whisk in the brown sugar. Cook, without stirring, for about 5 minutes or until the mixture is amber hued, the consistency of sand, and smells mildly nutty. Discard the vanilla pod and slowly whisk in the cream and milk over low heat until the sugar has dissolved. Remove from the heat and stir in the salt.

Bring a kettle of water to a boil and then set it aside. In a large bowl, whisk the egg yolks until they are pale and thickened, about 3 minutes. Add the cream mixture in a slow, steady stream, stirring constantly, until it's fully combined with the yolks. Strain the custard through a fine-mesh sieve into a bowl, then divide it evenly among the ramekins; each one should be about three-quarters full. Skim away any foam from the surface. Fill the baking pan with the hot water until it comes halfway up the sides of the ramekins. Cover the pan with foil and prick the foil with a fork. Bake for 45 minutes to 1 hour, or until the custards are set on the sides but still jiggle in the center. Transfer the ramekins to a wire rack and cool to room temperature. Cover each ramekin with plastic wrap and refrigerate at least 4 hours or up to overnight.

Make the caramel sauce: In a medium saucepan, heat the sugar and 2 tablespoons water over medium heat. Cook, swirling occasionally, until the sugar has dissolved. Increase the heat to medium-high and bring the liquid to a boil, gently swirling but never stirring it. If the sugar starts to crystallize, use a pastry brush dipped in water to wipe down the sides of the pan. After about five minutes, when the sugar is deep amber, remove it from the heat and whisk in the cream, butter, salt, tahini, and lemon juice. Set aside and let it cool to room temperature.

Before serving, bring the custards to room temperature. Sprinkle with flaky sea salt and serve topped with a dollop of whipped cream, a drizzle of caramel sauce, a sprinkle of toasted kasha, and sesame seeds.

For silky soft, pillowy dollops of whipped cream, a bowl, a whisk, and some elbow grease are your best options. It's easy to overdo it when using an electric mixer, resulting in overly stiff cream. When it comes to drizzling on the sauce, a delicate touch is key. Hold your spoon high and drip the sauce sparingly, serving any extra on the side.

THE
WINTER
TABLE

Rather than mourn winter's waning light, embrace the darkness with lush, moody décor and a warm, cozy vibe. Here, saturated gray linen, rumpled for added texture, serves as the backdrop for simple black ceramics, mismatched brass candlesticks, and a rambling arrangement of delicate flowers and ferns. A handmade touch—no matter how small—is the best way to add warmth to a table. For this meal at home with friends, I made ink-stained paper menu cards, adorning them with fragrant eucalyptus leaves. The overall feel is intimate, refined, and just a little decadent—like the perfect winter meal.

No.1
ON THE MENU

There are few things more festive than handwritten menus—even when they're not actually written by hand. Rather than hiring a calligrapher, select a scrolling script font and pop some pretty paper into your printer. Here, I used watercolor paper, tearing the edges and dabbing on watered-down ink, which bleeds to form a subtle, organic pattern.

No.2
WELL SEASONED

During citrus season, I love to flavor sea salt with a blend of zest and herbs. My recipe—which can be found on page 269—not only livens up roast fish or poultry, it also serves as a mouth-watering memento of the meal for guests to take home.

No.3
DARK MATTER

We change our wardrobes with the seasons, so why not our dishes? These days, investing in darker, moodier place settings for winter isn't particularly pricey. Chic—and cheap!—pieces can be found at stores like West Elm, CB2, and even IKEA.

No.4
LET THERE BE LIGHTS

A matched pair of candlesticks in the middle of your table can feel a little predictable. Instead, add visual interest—and set a casual, modern mood—with an odd-numbered grouping of vintage finds in a variety of heights and styles. Dark-colored tapers are an especially cozy touch on cold nights.

No.5
SPICE THINGS UP

Whole spices like nutmeg, all-spice, star anise, and cinnamon are too beautiful to keep hidden away in a drawer. And, especially during the holiday season, their sweet, warm scents feel festive without being overpowering. Here, I used the sculptural little gems to decorate a side table, alongside spicy sachets that guests can use at home to simmer mulled wine.

No.6
PRIZE RIBBONS

Words to live by: Never pass up a spool of pretty ribbon. If you keep some on hand, you'll find many lovely ways to use it, from holding together cutlery to binding bouquets—and, of course, tying up presents. Velvet varieties add elegant texture and subtle sheen to winter décor.

No.7
WRAP STAR

Gauzy linen, available at most fabric stores, can serve as a beautiful and unexpected alternative to wrapping paper. Simply cut or tear a large square—leaving the edges unfinished—place a gift in the center, and form a loose knot on top, tucking in a few green sprigs for a decorative touch.

No.8
CIRCLE OF LIFE

Get the look of a handmade wreath without the hassle of starting from scratch by purchasing the simplest evergreen option from your local market or nursery and embellishing it with seed pods, ornamental berries, feathers, sprigs, and other foraged finds.

No.9
SAY CHEESE

When artfully composed, a cheese plate can double as table décor. The most inviting platters feel abundant, so fill in vacant areas with fresh or dried fruit. The cheeses themselves should look natural and gooey. Break up any pristine wedges by hacking off a few messy chunks and let soft cheese sit at room temperature until properly runny.

SAUCES
AND EXTRAS

SALSA VERDE

This herb-packed classic livens up just about any protein. It's best when made the same day you plan to serve it.

½ cup (25 g) lightly packed fresh parsley
1 large handful fresh chives
5 sprigs fresh tarragon
1 clove garlic, chopped
1 anchovy
1 tablespoon capers
½ shallot, chopped
½ jalapeño, seeded and chopped (depending on your desired heat level, you can use a bit more or less)
1 tablespoon white wine vinegar
1 tablespoon whole-grain Dijon mustard
⅓ cup (75 ml) extra-virgin olive oil
2 lemons, preferably Meyer
Salt and freshly cracked pepper

In a food processor, pulse to combine the parsley, chives, tarragon, garlic, anchovy, capers, shallot, jalapeño, vinegar, and mustard. Slowly pour in the oil, pulsing to combine, until you have a smooth but textured sauce; if the sauce is too thick, loosen it with additional oil. Stir in the grated zest of 1 lemon and ¼ cup (60 ml) juice squeezed from 2 lemons. Season to taste with salt and pepper.

MAKES ¾ CUP (180 ML)

MACERATED
STRAWBERRIES

A dousing in lemon juice and sugar transforms lackluster berries by concentrating their sweetness.

---

1 pint (about 12 g) strawberries, trimmed and sliced
2 tablespoons granulated sugar
1 tablespoon fresh lemon juice

In a medium bowl, toss all of the ingredients together and let them sit at room temperature for 30 minutes, or until the strawberries release their juices. Use immediately.

MAKES 1 PINT (340 G)

LEMON-HERB VINAIGRETTE

Drizzle this dressing over grilled chicken or serve it alongside any delicate white fish. It can be made a day ahead but add the herbs just before serving.

⅓ cup (75 ml) extra-virgin olive oil
¼ cup (60 ml) fresh lemon juice (2 to 3 lemons)
Zest from 1 lemon
1 teaspoon salt
1 teaspoon honey
Pinch Aleppo pepper
2 tablespoons finely chopped fresh parsley
1 tablespoon finely chopped fresh cilantro

In a small bowl, whisk all of the ingredients together and taste for seasoning.

MAKES 1 CUP (240 ML)

WATERCRESS-PISTACHIO PESTO

Swirl this bright, vibrant blend into creamy soups or spread it on ricotta crostini.

⅓ cup (45 g) unsalted pistachios, toasted, plus more for garnish
1½ cups (60 g) packed watercress
¾ cup (45 g) packed fresh parsley
⅔ cup (165 ml) extra-virgin olive oil
⅓ cup (75 ml) lemon juice (about 2 lemons)
Zest of 1 lemon
Kosher salt

In a food processor, pulse the pistachios, watercress, and parsley until coarsely chopped, about ten pulses. Add the oil and lemon juice and process until a smooth, loose paste forms, about three 10-second pulses. Transfer the mixture to a bowl, stir in the lemon zest, and season with salt. Covered in the refrigerator, with a layer of olive oil on top, the pesto will last 3 to 4 days.

MAKES 2 CUPS (480 ML)

TZATZIKI SAUCE

The best way to meld the creamy and garlicky flavors is to make this sauce two to three hours before serving.

1 cup (240 ml) full-fat Greek yogurt
1 Kirby cucumber, seeded and finely chopped
1 small clove garlic, minced
A few fresh dill sprigs, finely chopped, plus more for garnish
A few fresh mint sprigs, leaves finely chopped
2 tablespoons fresh lemon juice
2 tablespoons extra-virgin olive oil
Salt and freshly cracked pepper

In a medium bowl, stir all of the ingredients together. Season to taste with salt and pepper. Garnish with a few pieces of torn dill. The sauce can be stored in the fridge for up to 2 days.

MAKES 2 CUPS (480 ML)

CHIMICHURRI

This Argentinean green sauce is traditionally served with grilled steak. It's best enjoyed the same day you make it.

3 cloves garlic
1 teaspoon kosher salt
½ cup (120 ml) extra-virgin olive oil
¼ cup (60 ml) white wine or champagne vinegar
1 lemon, zested and juiced
¼ teaspoon minced habanero chile
1 small shallot, finely chopped
½ cup (20 g) fresh cilantro, finely chopped
½ cup (25 g) fresh parsley, finely chopped
¼ cup (5 g) arugula, finely chopped
Freshly cracked pepper

Using a mortar and pestle, mash the garlic and salt to a paste. In a medium bowl, whisk together the oil, vinegar, lemon juice, lemon zest, habanero, and shallot. Stir in the garlic paste, cilantro, parsley, and arugula. Season with cracked pepper.

MAKES 2 CUPS (480 ML)

YOGURT-TAHINI SAUCE

This Mediterranean staple is great drizzled over grilled vegetables and makes a mean dip for flatbread.

¾ cup (180 ml) plain full-fat Greek yogurt
½ cup (120 ml) tahini
1 clove garlic, minced
3 tablespoons fresh lemon juice
2 tablespoons extra-virgin olive oil
Kosher salt

In a medium bowl, whisk together ⅓ cup (75 ml) water, the yogurt, tahini, garlic, lemon juice, and oil until smooth. Season with salt. Store in the refrigerator for up to 3 days.

MAKES 2 CUPS (480 ML)

PICKLED SHALLOTS

I like to keep a jar of these bright pink flavor bombs in my fridge. They add a zippy tang to tacos, grain salads, and roasted vegetable dishes. Apple cider vinegar can be substituted for the white wine vinegar here.

3 medium shallots, thinly sliced
⅓ cup (75 ml) white wine vinegar
1½ tablespoons sugar
1½ teaspoons kosher salt
½ serrano chile, minced (optional)

Place the shallot slices in a small bowl. In a small saucepan over medium-low heat, bring the vinegar, sugar, salt, and chile (if using) to a simmer, swirling the pan to help the sugar dissolve. Pour the pickling liquid over the shallots and let them cool to room temperature. Use immediately or store in an airtight container in the refrigerator for up to 2 weeks.

MAKES 1 CUP (100 G)

DUKKAH

I use this Middle Eastern spice and seed blend to add crunch and dimension to creamy soups. It's also delicious on hearty roasted vegetables.

¾ cup (95 g) unsalted pistachios
¼ cup (40 g) sesame seeds
2 tablespoons coriander seeds
2 tablespoons cumin seeds
1 teaspoon whole black peppercorns
1 teaspoon kosher salt

In a small skillet over medium-high heat, toast the pistachios for 2 minutes, until warm. Add the sesame seeds, coriander seeds, and cumin seeds. Continue to toast for 2 to 4 minutes, or until the seeds are fragrant. Transfer the mixture to a mini food processor, along with the peppercorns and salt. Pulse until the pistachios are coarsely chopped. The dukkah can be used immediately or stored in an airtight container in a cool place for up to 1 week.

MAKES ¾ CUP (95 G)

AVOCADO CREAM

If you want to make this dip in advance, top it with a very thin layer of water, cover it with plastic wrap, and pop it in the fridge. The water will prevent browning for 1 to 2 days.

2 ripe avocados, flesh roughly chopped
3 tablespoons fresh lime juice (from about 2 juicy limes)
1 teaspoon extra-virgin olive oil
½ teaspoon salt

In a mini food processor, blend all of the ingredients until they're smooth and creamy, with a silky, yogurt-like consistency.

MAKES 2 CUPS (480 ML)

CITRUS-HERB SALT

This vibrant, zippy salt is a seriously tasty way to finish fish, chicken, and pork.

2 cups (540 g) flaky sea salt
2 tablespoons finely minced fresh rosemary
2 tablespoons finely minced fresh sage
2 tablespoons finely minced fresh thyme
3 tablespoons orange zest
½ teaspoon dried lavender, crumbled (optional)

Preheat the oven to 225°F (110°C).

In a large bowl combine all of the ingredients, including the lavender (if using). Be sure to break up any clumps of zest.

Spread the mixture in a thin layer on a baking sheet lined with parchment.

Bake for 60 to 70 minutes, until the salt feels bone-dry to the touch. Allow it to cool completely before storing in an airtight container for up to 1 month.

MAKES 3 CUPS (810 G)

TOASTED BREAD CRUMBS

These crunchy nuggets add texture to everything from pasta to salads.

½ day-old baguette, cut into ¼-inch (6-mm) cubes
3 to 4 tablespoons extra-virgin olive oil
Pinch kosher salt

Preheat the oven to 350°F (175°C). In a food processor, pulse the bread until coarse crumbs form. Spread the bread crumbs on a baking sheet and toss with the oil and salt until evenly coated. Toast the crumbs until golden brown, tossing occasionally, 15 to 20 minutes. Once the bread crumbs have cooled completely, they can be stored in an airtight container at room temperature for 2 weeks.

MAKES 1 CUP (100 G)

PRESERVED LEMONS

The chopped rind of these cured fruits adds fermented punch to stews, seafood, grain salads, and dressings.

1 tablespoon coriander seeds
1 tablespoon fennel seeds
1 teaspoon peppercorns
1 teaspoon red pepper flakes
3 sprigs fresh thyme
1 bay leaf
1 cup (240 g) kosher salt
10 lemons, organic if possible

In a small sauté pan over medium heat, toast the coriander and fennel seeds until they begin to brown and are fragrant. In a medium bowl, mix together the spices with the peppercorns, pepper flakes, thyme, bay leaf, and salt.

Using a paring knife, trim the tips off 6 of the lemons. Then cut the lemons lengthwise into quarters, creating an X, leaving the lower quarter of the lemons intact. Place each lemon into the bowl.

Rub the exterior of each lemon individually with the salt mixture and fill the interior flesh until they are packed with salt, squeezing to release some juice. Once all the lemons are stuffed with the salt, place them into a 1-quart (960-ml) glass jar with an airtight seal. Pour any excess salt and accumulated juice over the lemons. Juice the remaining 4 lemons and pour in lemon juice to fully submerge the salted lemons, leaving some air space in the jar. Let this jar sit at room temperature until the rinds have softened, 3 weeks to 1 month. Once cured, the lemons will keep at room temperature for up to 3 months.

MAKES 6 LEMONS

SPICED CHICKPEAS

Serve these crunchy tidbits atop charred broccolini, scatter them on salads, or eat them straight up as a snack.

---

1 teaspoon cumin seeds, toasted and ground
1 teaspoon Aleppo pepper
¾ teaspoon kosher salt, plus more to taste
1 (15½-ounce/445-g) can unsalted chickpeas, drained, rinsed, and patted dry
Extra-virgin olive oil, for drizzling

Preheat the oven to 425°F (220°C). In a small bowl, mix together the cumin, pepper, and salt until combined.

Spread the chickpeas on a baking sheet and drizzle them generously with oil. Using the palm of your hand, roll the chickpeas in the oil until evenly coated. Sprinkle the spice mix over the chickpeas and toss them gently until evenly distributed.

Roast the chickpeas for 10 minutes, then shake the baking sheet and roast them for 10 minutes more. Turn off the oven and allow the chickpeas to sit in there for another 10 minutes—this will make them extra crispy. Remove from the oven and let them cool. Serve immediately.

MAKES ABOUT 1 CUP (100 G)

GRILLED FLATBREAD

Top these crisp, flavorful breads with pesto and grilled veggies or serve them with kabobs or other grilled meats.

1¼ teaspoons active dry yeast
1 pinch sugar
½ cup full-fat Greek yogurt
2½ tablespoons extra-virgin olive oil
2 cups all-purpose flour
1 teaspoon kosher salt
⅛ teaspoon baking soda
Canola oil, for greasing

In a small bowl, sprinkle the yeast over ¼ cup (60 ml) warm water (between 95°F [25°C] and 115°F [45°C]). Add a pinch of sugar and let the mixture stand until creamy, about 5 minutes.

In a separate small bowl, whisk the yogurt and olive oil together with 2 tablespoons water.

In the bowl of a stand mixer, whisk together the flour, salt, and baking soda. Add the yeast and yogurt mixtures and, using the dough hook attachment, mix on low speed until combined. Increase the speed to medium and beat until the dough is smooth and elastic, about 6 minutes.

Lightly grease a bowl with canola oil. Transfer the dough to the bowl and cover with a clean kitchen towel. Set aside in a warm place until the dough has doubled in size, 1½ to 2 hours.

Punch the dough down and either cover it with the towel and place it in a warm spot to rise for another hour or cover the bowl with plastic wrap and place in the refrigerator overnight. (The overnight rise will produce a lighter and more flavorful dough.)

On a lightly floured surface, stretch the dough into a ⅛-inch-thick rectangle. Heat an oiled stovetop griddle or your grill over medium-high heat and cook the flatbread until golden brown, 5 to 6 minutes per side.

SERVES 4 TO 6

PINEAPPLE SALSA

Sweet plus spice makes everything nice—from fish tacos to tortilla chips.

---

2 cups (330 g) finely chopped fresh pineapple
½ cup (65 g) finely chopped white onion
3 tablespoons fresh lime juice (from 2 limes)
¾ teaspoon minced habanero chile (or more, to taste)
½ teaspoon kosher salt
A few sprigs fresh mint, finely chopped
A couple sprigs fresh cilantro, finely chopped

In a small bowl, stir together all of the ingredients. Refrigerate in an airtight container for up to two days if not using immediately.

MAKES 2½ CUPS (425 G)

HORSERADISH BREAD CRUMBS

These every so slightly spicy crumbs brighten any braised or roasted meat.

½ cup (30 g) coarse bread crumbs
1 tablespoon extra-virgin olive oil
2 cloves garlic, finely chopped
1 cup (50 g) finely chopped flat-leaf parsley
2 tablespoons peeled and grated fresh horseradish
1 teaspoon finely grated lemon zest
1 teaspoon finely grated orange zest
Salt and freshly cracked pepper

In a small sauté pan, toast the bread crumbs with the oil over medium heat until golden brown, about 3 minutes. In a small bowl, combine the garlic, parsley, horseradish, zests, and bread crumbs, then season with salt and pepper.

MAKES 1½ CUPS (120 G)

TOASTED KASHA

Nutty, crunchy, and absolutely addictive, this buckwheat topping is fantastic sprinkled on yogurt or any creamy dessert.

---

2 tablespoons unsalted butter or coconut oil
1 cup (165 g) kasha
¼ teaspoon kosher salt

In a small saucepan, heat the butter over medium heat until melted. Add the kasha and salt and sauté, tossing continuously, until the grain releases a nutty fragrance and becomes golden brown, 5 to 7 minutes. Season with additional salt to taste and set aside to cool completely. Store in an airtight container at room temperature for up to a week.

MAKES ABOUT 1 CUP (180 G)

MY TOOLBOX

I'm not one for superfluous kitchen gadgets. To earn a place in my arsenal, a tool must serve a real purpose—and preferably more than one! These are the workhorses I reach for day after day.

MANDOLINE When you invest in a mandoline, vegetables that you never thought of eating raw—beets, sunchokes, zucchini—suddenly become salad material. The Japanese brand Benriner makes an inexpensive model that's beloved by chefs. I've used mine for more than a decade and it's still going strong.

MICROPLANE I don't know what I did before this handy piece of hardware came into my life—and it's not just for zesting! There's no better way to finely grate cheese and quickly puree garlic.

MINI FOOD PROCESSOR I use mine so much—for dressings, quick sauces, chimichurri and pesto—that I don't even bother to put it away. She sits out on my counter at all times!

CAST-IRON SKILLET No other pan delivers—and retains—heat more evenly. Keep it well seasoned and never get near it with soap. To clean, scrub it lightly with kosher salt and just a little water.

HALF SHEET PAN Also known as jelly-roll pans, these are a staple of professional kitchens for a reason: They're endlessly useful for roasting vegetables and meats, and, of course, making cookies.

SHARP KNIVES You really only need three: a paring knife for cutting vegetables; a serated knife for bread, tomatoes, and citrus; and a chef's knife for everything else. Rule of thumb: If your blade can't slice through a tomato skin, it needs to be sharpened.

PLASTIC SQUEEZE BOTTLE Used by chefs to create perfect sauce squiggles and soup swirls, these inexpensive squirters also work well for olive oil, delivering just the right drizzle for finishing a dish.

SPRITZ BOTTLE A fine mist of water instantly perks up herbs and delicate microgreens, which become waterlogged if submerged. Bonus: You can also use it for your orchids!

BLUNT-TIP TWEEZERS These little pinchers come in handy for fishing herb bundles or bay leaves out of soups or stews and carefully lifting the edge of a delicate fish fillet to check for doneness.

Y-SHAPED PEELER For much more than just removing skin from fruit and veg, this handy gizmo also delivers paper-thin wisps of hard cheese and perfect coils of shaved chocolate.

THERMOMETERS A digital, instant-read meat thermometer takes the guesswork out of roast chicken and other proteins, while a basic oven thermometer ensures you're actually cooking at the right temp.

TONGS These babies are like an extension of your hands—and I use mine so much that they might as well be! I prefer silicone-tipped models, which won't tear skin when flipping chicken or fish. They're also indispensable for spaghetti—for both removing it from the pot and twirling it on the plate.

BENCH SCRAPER Though designed for dough, this simple piece of metal is also the quickest means of tidying up your cutting board and scooping up tiny trimmings.

FLAT-ENDED WOODEN SPOON This classic does it all—stirring, flipping, scraping. I wouldn't know how to deglaze a pan without one.

PASTRY BRUSH Essential for applying egg wash to piecrusts and other flaky confections, mine actually gets more use painting olive oil onto bread for crostini.

BALLOON WHISK I'm a big proponent of hand-whipping cream and egg whites and this is the tool for the job. Its bulbous shape encourages fluffiness by drawing in extra air.

OFFSET SPATULA There's no better spreader for icing a cake, and it's also useful for leveling flour in a mixing cup and artfully smearing sauce onto a plate.

FINE-MESH SIEVE Scoop one up at a restaurant supply store and you'll use it to remove veggies from the blanching pot, drain small amounts of pasta, and strain stocks, citrus juice, and sauces.

MY PANTRY

I'm a big believer in cooking—and shopping—seasonally, so the contents of my kitchen vary widely from month to month. That said, there are a few things I always make sure to have on hand. Here, the all-year-round essentials I'd be lost without.

EXTRA-VIRGIN OLIVE OIL I always have at least two bottles within arm's reach: a less costly, mild-tasting variety for sautéing and roasting; and a brighter, grassier, pricier type—aka "the good stuff"—that I reserve for dressings and finishing drizzles.

CITRUS I can't cook without the punchy acidity of lemons and limes. To brighten roasted meats and provide a bracing counterpoint to sweets, I rely on their zest. And I use their juice to add zip to both the usual suspects—seafood and salads—and less expected dishes.

GOOD SALT More than any other ingredient, salt brings out the flavor in food—and chances are, you're not using enough! When I first started cooking with chefs for EyeSwoon, I was shocked by how much they were pouring into pasta water and showering on steaks. Regular table salt is highly processed and bleached, so I avoid it. Instead, I use kosher salt for cooking—layering it on multiple times over the course of a recipe. And I wouldn't know what to do without my flaky sea salt—my favorite is Maldon—for finishing.

VINEGAR Champagne and white wine vinegars are my go-tos for bright dressings. I use the raw, unfiltered apple cider variety to deglaze the pan and pull a sauce together for my roast chicken breasts. And red wine vinegar is just the thing for hearty Mediterranean salads.

FRESH HERBS In summer, I snip a wide variety from my garden, but during the cooler months I lean heavily on parsley. Widely available and hearty enough to keep for days in the fridge, it's a real workhorse. Instead of hacking away at it, which can bruise the leaves, pile your parsley into a tight bunch and make clean, concise cuts.

ALLIUMS Where would we be without garlic, onions, leeks, and shallots? These versatile aromatics are the base upon which we build flavor. And they're also delicious in their own right. I love the sweetness of whole roasted shallots, the sharp bite of pickled red onion, and the gorgeously mellow flavor of garlic confit.

TAHINI Made from ground sesame seeds, this paste is essential to Middle Eastern dishes like hummus and baba ghanoush. In my kitchen, it's most often used as the base of a highly addictive salad dressing and a deliciously nutty sauce for cooked veg.

NUTS I always have hazelnuts, almonds, pistachios, and pine nuts in my fridge or freezer—which is the best way to keep them fresh. Roasted and chopped, they're the fastest, tastiest way to add crunchy texture to salads, vegetables, and grain dishes. And let's not forget their importance in my beloved pestos!

MUSTARD The varieties are endless, but my MVPs are Dijon and whole grain. A multi-purpose flavor booster, mustard wakes up a wide variety of sauces and salad dressing and also serves as a thickener and emulsifier for vinaigrette.

CHEESE I appreciate good Parm as much as any Italian-American girl, but when it comes to cheese, my true love is pecorino, which is sharper and saltier. When the situation calls for something creamier, I reach for feta—preferably the Bulgarian variety, which is saltier and smoother than its Greek cousin.

FRESH CHILES When I was growing up, dried red pepper flakes were really the only option for adding spice to a dish. These days, I'm much more likely to reach for fresh habaneros, Fresnos, or jalapeños. Yes, cooking with hot peppers can be scary—don't touch your eyes!—but you can't beat their clean heat. Ditch the seeds to control the burn, or leave them in if you want it hot hot hot!

OLIVES AND CAPERS These are the ultimate flavor bombs. Salt-packed capers are the most prized—just remember to soak them a little before using. And when it comes to olives, I'm a sucker for the brilliant green Castelvetrano variety, whether tossed into a kale salad or chopped into a savory gremolata.

MY LITTLE BLACK BOOK

What good is pretty food without a pretty plate—and napkin, and fork, and glass to sit beside it? I've spent countless hours shopping and scouring the Web for just the right décor and tabletop treasures. Here, my favorite sources for pottery, linens, glassware, and more.

SPECK AND STONE

speckandstone.com
Their beautifully minimal, handmade ceramics are my everyday dishes in Amagansett.

JONO PANDOLFI

jonopandolfi.com
Many top New York chefs commission dinnerware for their restaurants from this master ceramicist.

HENRY STREET STUDIO

henrystreetstudio.com
A favorite of prop stylists, this uniquely textured, highly coveted pottery is produced by a mother-daughter team.

CLAM LAB

clamlab.com
With gorgeous glazes and organic-feeling forms, designer Clair Catillaz's platters and vessels are true showstoppers.

ERIC BONNIN

ericbonninceramics.com
I often pull out Bonnin's hand-dipped, sandy-hued "Kam" stoneware for beachy summer meals.

MUD AUSTRAILIA

mudaustralia.com
This handmade porcelain comes in a wide range of hues. Bonus: It's dishwasher-, microwave-, and oven-safe.

STAUB

staubusa.com
Enameled cast-iron cookware that's pretty enough to display. Their matte-black Dutch oven is my personal fave.

SUR LA TABLE

surlatable.com
My go-to source for kitchen basics. The best selection of baking pans, cooking gadgets, and more.

WILLIAMS-SONOMA

williams-sonomainc.com
The place to invest in your culinary workhorses, from All-Clad and Le Creuset cookware to mixers and food processors galore.

ETSY
etsy.com
I often hunt this virtual wonderland for vintage copper pieces, glassware, and cutting boards to add to my collections.

NOT PERFECT LINEN
etsy.com/shop/notPERFECTLINEN
This Lithuania-based family business turns out gorgeous linen tablecloths and napkins in a variety of subtle hues.

ROUGH LINEN
roughlinen.com
I love their European-style linen table runners, napkins, and aprons, which have a lovely homespun texture.

ABC CARPET & HOME
abchome.com
This New York City store sells the most beautiful tabletop, kitchen, and home goods. The displays always send me swooning.

FOOD52
food52.com/shop
A cook's dream, with a huge and carefully selected range of tabletop, kitchen, home, and pantry goods.

BLACK CREEK MERCANTILE & TRADING CO.
blackcreekmt.com
Handmade artisanal wooden bowls, spoons, and boards, which make gorgeous cheese platters.

MARCH
marchsf.com
A tightly edited, impeccable selection of chic, high-end tabletop, glassware, and kitchen goods.

ALDER & CO.
alderandcoshop.com
With outposts in Portland, Oregon, and Upstate New York, this shop features beautiful home décor and ceramics to adorn your table.

SALT HOUSE MARKET
salthousemkt.com
Everything from kitchen appliances to dishes to hard-to-find spices, it's a one-stop shop for design-minded foodies.

SPARTAN SHOP
spartan-shop.com
My go-to online resource for tabletop accessories—from wine keys to candleholders to hand-forged brass serving spoons.

QUITOKEETO
quitokeeto.com
Blogger and cookbook writer Heidi Swanson's online emporium features beautiful, limited-edition pieces that sell out fast.

ANTHROPOLOGIE
anthropologie.com
I often turn to this beloved chain for their great selection of minimal flatware, delicate glassware, and copper baking tools.

CB2
cb2.com
Their Marta glassware is clean-lined, perfectly scaled, and remarkably inexpensive. It's a staple in both of my homes.

CRATE & BARREL
crateandbarrel.com
I rely on their flour-sack kitchen towels and huge selection of well-priced wineglasses.

IKEA
ikea.com
Gems at this Scandi superstore include glass carafes, simple serving platters, and lidded kitchen storage containers.

WEST ELM
westelm.com
This national chain is based in Dumbo—just like I am! Their matte-finish Scape plates are my everyday dishes in the city.

ACKNOWLEDGMENTS

Abrams, you offered this dreamer a platform to share what I always considered to be my intuition for the delicious. This process has been about far more than cooking—in collecting recipes and memories, I have learned to trust my own creative instincts. I am truly grateful for the support.

Camaren Subhiyah, my incredible editor, you gently pushed me in times of doubt and steered me back on course when I drifted. I am so thankful for the opportunity to bring this book to life with you. Thank you for your unwavering belief in me and this project.

Johnny Miller, I could not have asked for a finer creative collaborator. Our shot list was ambitious, to say the least, and you captured it all with poise and sophistication. Your energy on set made our fourteen-hour days possible! Thank you for your willingness to jump into my mayhem.

Rebecca Jurkevich, you're a rare bird: a true talent with zero ego and some serious culinary magic. Thank you for making my food look ridiculously swoon-worthy. You can manage the playlist anytime!

Rebecca Bartoshesky, my shepherd in creating beauty, you pulled it all together visually. Your talent, eye, and sense of style is simply impeccable. Each and every prop was a gem.

Tyna, Will, Justin, and Jenna, our days on set were long and hard but also a lot of fun. Thank you for your manpower and your willingness to dive right in.

Karen Robinovitz, without you, this project would not exist. Thank you for making a dream a reality and for your continued belief in me.

Nicole Tourtelot, I likely drove you insane throughout this journey but I could not have kept on track without your steady guidance and reassurance that I am not crazy and I am not alone.

Rob Magnotta and the Edge Reps team, I am so grateful for your friendship, advice, and calming support as I entered into uncharted territory.

Jenny Comita, I love that we conceived the concept of this book together from day one. Thank you for helping me express all that I wanted to say. I could have never imagined this journey without you. You were simply invaluable to this book.

Natalie Goel, we went from remote collaborators to fast friends. Thank you for lending your wise words and constant curiosity to this book. We sure did learn a lot together.

Rebecca Flint Marx, I am beyond grateful for your professionalism. Thank you for whipping my recipes into shape.

Amanda Jane Jones, you mapped out this book right from the initial proposal and did such a brilliant job, it's hardly changed since then. Grace and beauty pours onto every page you design.

Dawn Perry, I simply adore you. You were my entrance into this journey. I am ever so thankful for having you lead the charge.

Molly Shuster, I would be lost without your careful precision in the kitchen. I learned SO much from you.

Cara Nicoletti, we had such a blast and made such a mess! You are truly a badass. Your belief in my flavors helped me embrace my instincts.

Pearl Jones and Tyna Hoang, I cannot thank you enough for helping me perfect each and every recipe, sometimes multiple times.

Evan Kalman and Eden Grinshpan, I thank you for lending me your impeccable palates.

Jordana Mostel, I would be lost without you. This book could not exist without all of your behind-the-scenes support and organization.

Jenna Saraco, your guidance on visual direction was invaluable—I could not have been on set without your support!

Sarah Elliott, Chloe Crespi, and Winnie Au, what we have built together through EyeSwoon paved the way for this book. Thank you for helping me establish a beautiful vision.

Jenny Huang, the recipes we developed together for ES made their way into this book. I am ever so grateful to you.

Andrea Gentl, Kim Ficaro, Christine Muhlke, Nicole Franzen, Aran Goyoaga, and Karen Mordechai, I called on you often throughout this process—thank you for your guidance and endless advice.

Libby and Kelsey of Tandem Entertainment, gracious thanks for your support in growing my brand and encouraging me to dream big.

Jenné Lombardo, you gave me the push I so desperately needed.

Tali Magal, you see me, always. Having your eyes, your magic, your love all over this book means the world to me.

So much gratitude to all those who generously loaned beautiful things to make this book so darn purdy—**Ulla Johnson, Warm, Tibi, Club Monaco, Rough Linen, Staub, Not Perfect Linen, Speck and Stone, Food52, ABC Home, Becca PR, Blackcreek Mercantile, Spartan Shop, Milk & Clay, Salt House Market, Mud Australia, and Mondays.**

Pete Maiden and the entire Convicts video crew, thanks for capturing the making of a cookbook!

Coleman, your tunes! Obsessed with my cookbook playlist—thanks for keeping us moving.

Amber Waves Farm, Balsam Farms, and Good Water Farms, your beautiful ingredients, grown locally with such love, made my meals possible. I am ever grateful to be a part of your community.

Laura and Fabio of Westwind Orchard, I love you both so much. Thank you for your friendship and extreme generosity in opening your beautiful farm and breathtaking barn for our fall shoot.

Susan Spungen, thank you for feeding us and lending me your swoony copper cookware.

Fodder Fox Farm, the winter florals and wall garland were absolutely swoon-worthy, many thanks, Taylor!

Julie and Dan Resnick of FeedFeed, thank you for offering your home for summer crabbing.

Leilani Bishop, Jack and Cassius Luber, and Rosie and Mike Densen, thanks for making the summer paella beach scene possible.

Nancy Jo Iacoi, I am forever grateful for your discriminating eye to help me edit imagery.

Dan Kluger, Jody Williams, Anna Klinger, Johnathan Adler, as well as the team at Franny's and Roberta's, your food awakened my palate and inspired many recipes in this book. I am grateful beyond measure.

Victor, you are the love of my life and my best friend. You have supported my every whim with an unwavering belief in me. You nudge me along—and clean up my kitchen messes. Thank you for always looking at me like I am magic.

Jivan, you are the greatest joy life has offered me. Because of you, I am more conscious, wiser, softer, slower. My heart overflows with love and pride in all that you are. Your creative mind and fearlessness astonish me. Thank you for being my mirror.

Mom, my love of beauty is a gift I inherited from you. Thank you. This book is without doubt an extension of all that I absorbed growing up.

My Family and Sweet Friends . . .

You have lent me your ears, your bellies, your laughter, your comfort, and so many memories from countless gatherings. Each of you (you know who you are) have likely eaten everything in this book at some point over the years and have helped foster my creativity in some way. Thank you for your honesty when my meals are not so swoony and for your praise when they are. I love you!

EyeSwoon readers, you offered me the ability to play, to trust myself, and to get creative. Thank you for believing in me and for swooning with me.

Editor: Camaren Subhiyah

Designer: Amanda Jones

Production Manager: Rebecca Westall

Library of Congress Control Number: 2016960601

ISBN: 978-1-4197-2652-1

Printed and bound in China

15 14 13 12 11 10 9 8

Abrams books are available at special discounts when
purchased in quantity for premiums and promotions as
well as fundraising or educational use. Special editions
can also be created to specification. For details, contact
specialsales@abramsbooks.com or the address below.

ABRAMS The Art of Books
195 Broadway, New York, NY 10007
abramsbooks.com